THE ART OF WOODWORKING

RESTORING ANTIQUES

THE ART OF WOODWORKING

RESTORING ANTIQUES

TIME-LIFE BOOKS
ALEXANDRIA, VIRGINIA

ST. REMY PRESS
MONTREAL • NEW YORK

THE ART OF WOODWORKING was produced by
ST. REMY PRESS

PUBLISHER	Kenneth Winchester
PRESIDENT	Pierre Léveillé
Series Editor	Pierre Home-Douglas
Series Art Director	Francine Lemieux
Senior Editor	Marc Cassini
Editor	Andrew Jones
Art Directors	Normand Boudreault, Michel Giguère
Designers	Hélène Dion, Jean-Guy Doiron, François Daxhelet, François Longpré
Picture Editor	Christopher Jackson
Writers	John Dowling, David Simon
Research Assistant	Adam Van Sertima
Contributing Illustrators	Gilles Beauchemin, Michel Blais, Ronald Durepos, Michael Stockdale, James Thérien
Administrator	Natalie Watanabe
Production Manager	Michelle Turbide
Coordinator	Dominique Gagné
System Coordinator	Eric Beaulieu
Photographer	Robert Chartier
Proofreader	Garet Markvoort
Indexer	Christine M. Jacobs

Time-Life Books is a division of Time Life Inc.,
a wholly owned subsidary of
THE TIME INC. BOOK COMPANY

TIME-LIFE INC.

President and CEO	John M. Fahey
Editor-in-Chief	John L. Papanek

TIME-LIFE BOOKS

President	John D. Hall
Vice-President, Director of Marketing	Nancy K. Jones
Managing Editor	Roberta Conlan
Director of Design	Michael Hentges
Director of Editorial Operations	Ellen Robling
Consulting Editor	John R. Sullivan
Vice-President, Book Production	Marjann Caldwell
Production Manager	Marlene Zack
Quality Assurance Manager	James King

THE CONSULTANTS

Paul McGoldrick owns and operates Pianoforte Inc., a piano restoration company in Montreal, Quebec. He is responsible for the maintenance and concert preparation of the pianos used by the Montreal Symphony Orchestra and the National Arts Center Orchestra in Ottawa, Ontario.

Giles Miller-Mead taught advanced cabinetmaking at Montreal technical schools for more than ten years. A native of New Zealand, he has worked as a restorer of antique furniture.

Marc A. Williams is President of The American Conservation Consortium in Fremont, New Hampshire. He studied at Winterthur Museum in Delaware and later founded the Furniture Conservation Program at the Smithsonian Institution. He is the author of *Keeping It All Together: The Preservation and Care of Historic Furniture*, published by The Ohio Antique Review.

Restoring antiques.
p. cm. — (The Art of woodworking)
Includes index.
ISBN 0-8094-9929-0
1. Furniture–Repairing. 2. Woodwork. I. Time-Life Books.
II. Series.
TT199.R47 1995
749'. 1'0288—dc20   94-49006
                                              CIP

Trade Edition ISBN: 0-7370-0302-2

For information about any Time-Life book,
please call 1-800-621-7026, or write:
Reader Information
Time-Life Customer Service
P.O. Box C-32068
Richmond, Virginia
23261-2068

CONTENTS

Ron Sheetz and Al Levitan restore
LONGFELLOW'S FURNITURE

As conservators of wooden objects for the National Park Service, we are often in the enviable position of examining and treating some of our nation's most significant artifacts. The primary purpose of our work is not to return an object to its original appearance, but long-term preservation, slowing the rate of future deterioration. Before treatment begins, we examine the object and record pertinent information, such as the type of finish, adhesives, construction techniques, and wood species. Tool marks on the wood surface, hardware fabrication techniques, even nail and screw type, all help to date the object. We look for clues that shed light on the maker and user of the artifact as well as the changes it has undergone. Often the information found through our examination can help establish provenance and authenticity, and ultimately improve the interpretation and restoration of the object.

Recently, we have worked on a Herter Brothers cabinet from Teddy Roosevelt's Sagamore Hill home, tools and equipment used in steam-era railroading, a Sheraton chair donated to the White House collection, and a humble shaving mirror once used by Abraham Lincoln. In our lab right now are a number of pieces of furniture from the Cambridge, Massachusetts home of Henry Wadsworth Longfellow. The 235-year-old Georgian structure was used by George Washington as his military headquarters between 1775 and 1776, a connection with the past that was a major reason Longfellow purchased the house in 1843. Longfellow and his wife were antiquarians and collectors of Americana, and among the 35,000 objects and documents in the their collection are beautiful examples of Queen Anne, Chippendale, and Federal-style furniture. Two of their Renaissance Revival-style chairs are shown in the photo at left.

Today, many of these pieces are in considerably worse condition than when they were purchased by the Longfellows a century and a half ago. The primary reason is what we in the conservation field refer to as "inherent vice." The furniture, for the most part made from white oak, was assembled from partially green or unseasoned wood, using poor construction techniques. As a result, we are faced with a multitude of problems such as warped boards, separated moldings, split panels, doors that won't close, and drawers that won't open.

Fixing these problems presents many choices. We must rectify the condition while achieving long-term stability. At the same time we have to balance respect for the integrity of the object and the preservation of original materials with the need to present an appearance close to that seen by its original owners. That's part of what makes our jobs so challenging—and so appealing.

Ron Sheetz (left) *and Al Levitan restore antique furniture at the Division of Conservation at Harpers Ferry Center, a multi-lab facility in West Virginia that functions as a central conservation resource for the U.S. National Park Service.*

Gregory J. Landrey on the
CONSERVATION ETHIC

When hand, tool, or brush are brought to an antique, we need to strike a challenging balance: to serve the aesthetic and functional needs of the furniture while not diminishing evidence of original fabrication, age, and use.

The terms restoration and conservation are used almost interchangeably today, which can cause some confusion. Essentially, conservation is the work done to preserve an object while restoration denotes a return to some previous condition. Restoration is a specific activity that falls under the larger umbrella of conservation. The task of the practitioner in this field is to take responsibility for preserving the history and nature of the object while carrying out necessary treatment.

Whether a restoration project is being carried out in a private shop or a museum studio, the intrinsic value of the "antique" should come first. Admittedly, there are differences in the objectives of a project done for private use or for display in a museum exhibit. The antique in the home may see daily use while a museum object normally does not. This will affect the treatment plans of the conservator or restorer. However, the innate qualities of the piece of furniture are still to be respected as treatment decisions are made.

Blemishes, patterns of wear, out-of-plane boards, old surfaces, and even some missing parts and pieces may best be accepted as part of the history and interest of the piece rather than a liability. In restoration, we often can be tempted to do too much, only to regret it later. It can be a puzzle to know where to begin work. Proceeding with appropriate restraint and treating the antique with the respect it deserves seems like a good place to start.

Those of us who conserve, restore, and enjoy antique furniture find something of value in them that goes beyond that which we could make or buy new. It is the preservation of the work of previous craftsmen that is our goal. Antiques are a cultural legacy, and the significance of a piece of furniture may be its association with our great-great-grandparents or with a legendary cabinetmaker, both of which can be equally valid. It is my hope that when I work on an antique that the furniture itself, its makers, and its history are brought to life while my efforts go largely unnoticed.

Great pride should be taken in the quality of workmanship, a lesson I learned years ago training in the cabinet shop of Corner Cupboard Antiques in Stafford, Pennsylvania. The skill of the practitioner working on antiques must be of the highest level since we are affecting the work and history of others, not something of our own making. It is the sensitivity of the restorer's and conservator's hand skills that are the benchmark by which he or she will be judged.

Gregory J. Landrey is a senior furniture conservator at the Henry Francis du Pont Winterthur Museum in Delaware.

George Frank recalls
MATCHING THE PATINA OF AGE

A Mr. Carl Black was president of an obscure association of interior decorators in the early 1950s, with offices on Upper Lexington Avenue in New York. This important personage asked me to meet him there one afternoon. After keeping me waiting a half hour, Mr. Black greeted me with a well-practised smile, and ordered me to "Have a seat, Frank."

Black continued, "As you know, Christmas is soon here, and I am working for the most important people in the country. But I am not sending them cards! Not me. I am sending them gifts. Take a look at this!" I looked. "This is not a table, this is a winestand, and, believe it or not, this one comes from Thomas Jefferson's home, Monticello. Thomas parked his guest in one of the comfortable chairs and rested his wineglass on this little table."

Then came Black's question. "Can you make me twelve copies of this table in five weeks?" The table was made of plain American cherry, of which I happened to have a large stock on hand. "Yes," I said, "I can make the twelve copies on time."

"You've got the order," said Black, "and my secretary will confirm it. Do you need to take the model?"

"I would not do the job without it, Sir."

"Okay, take it, but take good care of it. You should know that if it were made of solid gold, it would not be worth more."

He continued: "Do a good job! I know you cannot match the patina of age, but do your best."

I did my best, and so, shortly before December, my truckman delivered to Mr. Black his authentic winestand from the Thomas Jefferson estate, plus twelve copies.

Soon, I began receiving repeated calls notifying me that Mr. Black would like to see Mr. Frank. Each time, my secretary answered that I was out of town, or otherwise unable to meet. I never saw Mr. Black again, nor did I ever tell him which of the thirteen winestands was the original. As far as I know, Mr. Black died without knowing to whom he gave the original, or if, indeed, he ever did.

George Frank ran one of Europe's top cabinetmaking studios in Paris before moving to the United States in 1940. His articles and tales about the craft of replicating antique finishes have appeared in numerous magazines, and he is the author of Adventures In Wood Finishing, *published by The Taunton Press.*

RESTORING BASICS

Restoring antiques is a rewarding and economical way to fill a home with fine furniture, but for many restorers, the process leads to a deeper experience, of forging links to the past. Whether firming up a wobbly joint or uncovering the natural wood grain under multiple layers of paint, returning a piece of timeworn furniture to its original condition is like traveling back in time to discover the methods of a woodworker from another generation. You can appreciate the skill used—and perhaps learn from any mistakes the builder made.

The main challenge of furniture restoration is to repair what needs to be fixed without destroying this link with the past. Most projects involve a balancing act between authenticity and function: You will want to remain faithful to the age and style of the original, while preserving its usefulness. There are no absolute rules about how to proceed. A museum curator who comes into possession of an antique with historic importance is concerned first and foremost with preserving the piece—whatever its condition—for future generations to study and enjoy. But the priorities are different if you simply want to return an old chair or table to personal service. For a chair with a cracked seat, loose joints, a damaged finish, and a couple of broken legs, for example, the prescription is sim-

The before-and-after effects of restoration are displayed in a single chair in this display piece from Minotaur Workshop of Montreal, Canada.

ple: You will need to effect a complete restoration. For a table with no structural damage, you may be able to restore the piece with just a thorough cleaning and waxing. A gallery of useful restoration tools opens on the next page. Tips for cleaning and caring for old furniture appear on page 17.

One cause for uncertainty among amateur restorers is establishing the worth of a piece. Making careless repairs to a valuable piece—bracing loose joinery with hardware, for example, or stripping off the original finish—can substantially reduce its value. It is a good idea to learn all you can about antique furniture from dealers, exhibitions, museums, books, and magazines. An illustrated guide to some of the major furniture styles of the last four centuries begins on page 18. While you are not likely to stumble across a 400-year-old piece at a farm auction, it is useful to know how different styles relate to each other and how they evolved.

As a rule of thumb, the safest course of action is to use the least intrusive remedy for a particular problem. For a very tricky repair—or a particularly valuable antique—consider enlisting the help of a professional restorer. For example, many antiques from the Colonial era were originally painted and an experienced restorer can strip the more recent paint layers while leaving the original ones intact.

For most restoration projects, a well-equipped shop is a must: a full range of clamps for gluing loose and broken joints, and a wide selection of stains and finishes to match the coloring and sheen typically found on older furniture. Since restoring often involves stripping and refinishing, it is essential that the room be well ventilated.

INVENTORY OF TOOLS

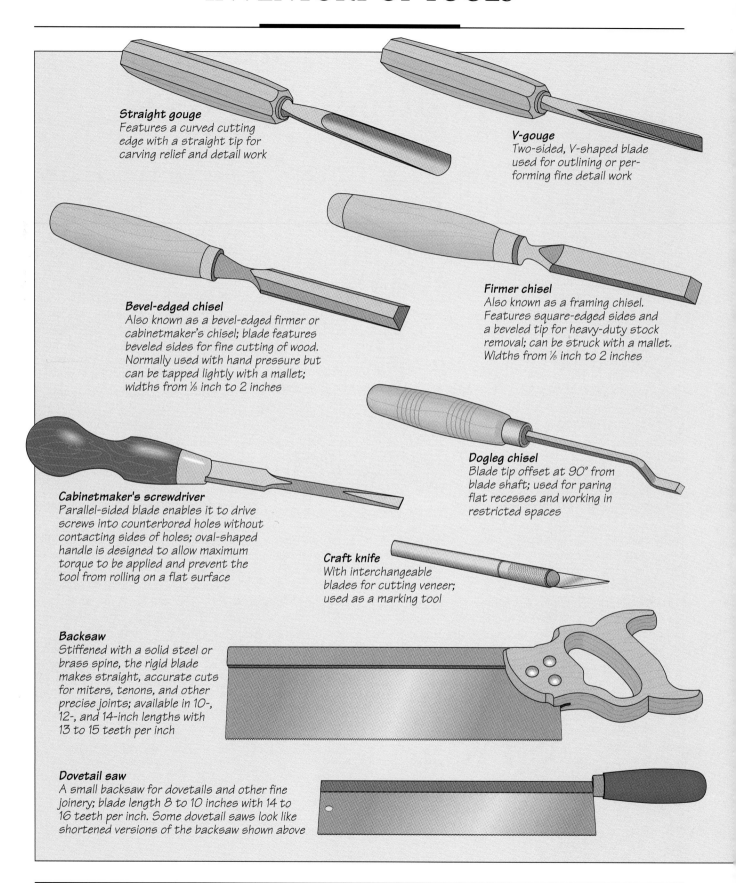

Straight gouge
Features a curved cutting edge with a straight tip for carving relief and detail work

V-gouge
Two-sided, V-shaped blade used for outlining or performing fine detail work

Bevel-edged chisel
Also known as a bevel-edged firmer or cabinetmaker's chisel; blade features beveled sides for fine cutting of wood. Normally used with hand pressure but can be tapped lightly with a mallet; widths from ⅛ inch to 2 inches

Firmer chisel
Also known as a framing chisel. Features square-edged sides and a beveled tip for heavy-duty stock removal; can be struck with a mallet. Widths from ⅛ inch to 2 inches

Cabinetmaker's screwdriver
Parallel-sided blade enables it to drive screws into counterbored holes without contacting sides of holes; oval-shaped handle is designed to allow maximum torque to be applied and prevent the tool from rolling on a flat surface

Dogleg chisel
Blade tip offset at 90° from blade shaft; used for paring flat recesses and working in restricted spaces

Craft knife
With interchangeable blades for cutting veneer; used as a marking tool

Backsaw
Stiffened with a solid steel or brass spine, the rigid blade makes straight, accurate cuts for miters, tenons, and other precise joints; available in 10-, 12-, and 14-inch lengths with 13 to 15 teeth per inch

Dovetail saw
A small backsaw for dovetails and other fine joinery; blade length 8 to 10 inches with 14 to 16 teeth per inch. Some dovetail saws look like shortened versions of the backsaw shown above

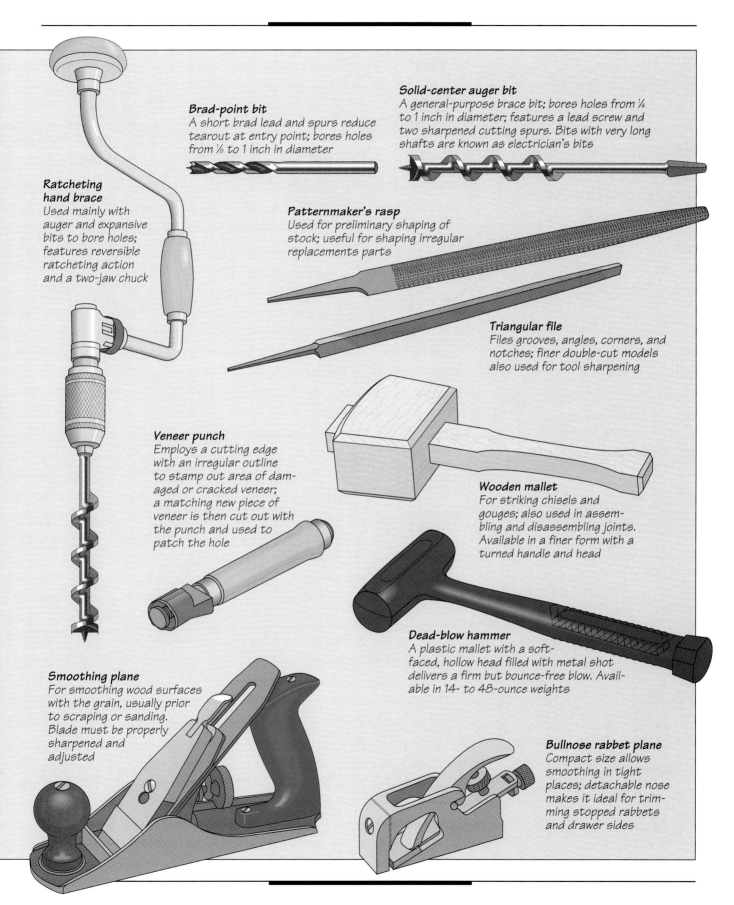

Brad-point bit
A short brad lead and spurs reduce tearout at entry point; bores holes from ⅛ to 1 inch in diameter

Solid-center auger bit
A general-purpose brace bit; bores holes from ¼ to 1 inch in diameter; features a lead screw and two sharpened cutting spurs. Bits with very long shafts are known as electrician's bits

Ratcheting hand brace
Used mainly with auger and expansive bits to bore holes; features reversible ratcheting action and a two-jaw chuck

Patternmaker's rasp
Used for preliminary shaping of stock; useful for shaping irregular replacements parts

Triangular file
Files grooves, angles, corners, and notches; finer double-cut models also used for tool sharpening

Veneer punch
Employs a cutting edge with an irregular outline to stamp out area of damaged or cracked veneer; a matching new piece of veneer is then cut out with the punch and used to patch the hole

Wooden mallet
For striking chisels and gouges; also used in assembling and disassembling joints. Available in a finer form with a turned handle and head

Dead-blow hammer
A plastic mallet with a soft-faced, hollow head filled with metal shot delivers a firm but bounce-free blow. Available in 14- to 48-ounce weights

Smoothing plane
For smoothing wood surfaces with the grain, usually prior to scraping or sanding. Blade must be properly sharpened and adjusted

Bullnose rabbet plane
Compact size allows smoothing in tight places; detachable nose makes it ideal for trimming stopped rabbets and drawer sides

Sliding bevel
Can be adjusted to any angle, then locked into position to transfer or measure the angle

Dial calipers
Makes precise inside and outside measurements; graduated in 1/100-inch increments

Needle-nose pliers
The very fine tip of these pliers make them handy for extracting small nails from damaged joints

Contour gauge
Indispensable for copying old mold-ings and turned objects, the small pins are pressed straight into the shaped object and adopt its form

Screw extractor
Screws with worn-out heads can be removed by driving this tool into their shafts then un-screwing them

Needle-point glue injector
A syringe-type glue applicator for inserting glue into joints and under veneer

Web clamp
Also known as a strap clamp; used to apply pressure in more than one direction, such as when clamping four chair legs at once. Typically features a 1-inch wide, 15-foot-long nylon band with a ratcheting buckle and four corner fittings

Electric glue pot
Maintains hide glue at correct tempera-ture; hide glue is often recommended for repairing antiques because it is a reversible adhesive

HIDE GLUE

CARING FOR ANTIQUES

Your first "repair" act to a newly acquired antique should be a thorough cleaning. In many cases, the original finish will be in better shape than you first suspected, saving hours of stripping and refinishing. As the chart directly below suggests, you should use the mildest cleaning agent that gets the job done. Start with water and soap, only using stronger cleaners when necesssary or to spot-clean problem areas. Before using any cleaner on a wood surface, make sure it will not harm the finish by rubbing a small amount on an inconspicuous area. Even a water-based cleaner can damage wood if it is not wiped off quickly. For best results, clean one small section at a time and work with two lint-free cloths, using one to apply the cleaner and the other to wipe the surface dry. Always wipe a cleaner on and off in the direction of the grain.

With the plethora of furniture care products on the market, maintaining antiques can be very confusing. In fact, there is very little that you need do to improve the protection provided by a properly applied finish. The most important consideration is to make sure a piece is protected from wear and tear, and excessive heat and light. Although waxes and polishes offer limited protection, it is best to keep furniture out of direct sunlight and any areas that can get very hot, such as next to fireplaces or in attics. You can protect a highly valued antique from the wood movement that results from seasonal humidity fluctuations by controlling the relative humidity with a humidifier or a dehumidifier, as needed. Refer to the chart below as a guide to caring for your furniture.

CLEANING ANTIQUES

CLEANER	APPLICATIONS	PROCEDURE
Vacuum	All furniture, especially carved surfaces	Use soft brush attachment. For loose veneer and upholstery, cover end with a piece of window screen taped on all four edges.
Distilled water and mild soap	All furniture	Dampen a soft, lint-free cloth with water and soap, work on a small area at a time, drying immediately with a clean cloth. Repeat with clean distilled water to remove soap residue, then dry.
Mineral spirits, paint thinner (preferably odorless)	All furniture, except oiled finishes	Test on finish in an inconspicuous spot. Removes wax; solvent will evaporate, so rinsing is unnecessary.
Naphtha; benzene	All furniture, except oiled finishes	A more volatile version of mineral spirits, better for lifting oil and grease. Follow same procedure as mineral spirits.

If more powerful cleaners are needed or bare unfinished patches of wood are exposed, the antique should be referred to a professional restorer or refinished depending on its value.

CARE OF ANTIQUE FINISHES

FURNITURE CARE PRODUCT	APPLICATIONS
Paste wax	Will provide a wear-resistant shine for one to three years, or less if furniture is exposed to daily use.
Furniture polish	Based on petroleum-distillate solvents, such as paint thinner and kerosene, with scent added (usually lemon). Cleans well but shine disappears in a few days as product evaporates; collects dirts while wet. Dissolves paste wax.
Any treatment containing linseed oil	Traps dust and dirt, and darkens over time; requires strong solvents to remove, which can damage the original finish. Not recommended for antiques.

Maintaining antiques
Dust all wood furniture regularly, sweeping a feather duster lightly over the surface along the grain. Dust is an abrasive and can scratch wood surfaces if it is rubbed too hard. Despite the claims made by the makers of furniture waxes and polishes, such products are not necessary to maintain a finish. Some can actually do more harm than good. Most furniture polishes actually dissolve paste wax and collect dust and dirt while they are still wet.

A GALLERY OF FURNITURE STYLES

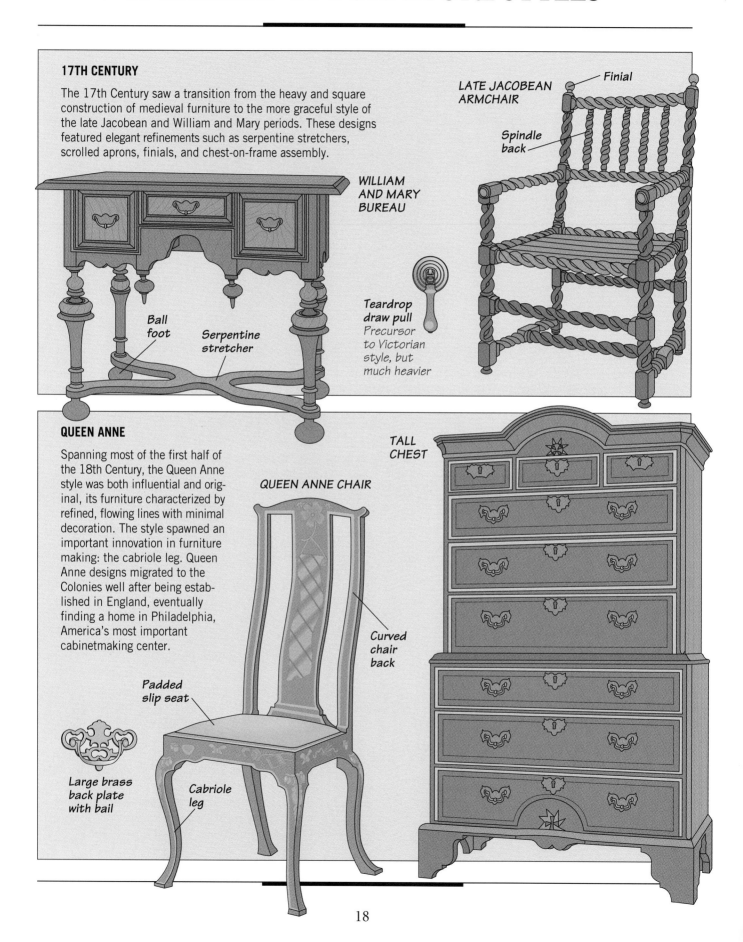

17TH CENTURY

The 17th Century saw a transition from the heavy and square construction of medieval furniture to the more graceful style of the late Jacobean and William and Mary periods. These designs featured elegant refinements such as serpentine stretchers, scrolled aprons, finials, and chest-on-frame assembly.

LATE JACOBEAN ARMCHAIR

Finial

Spindle back

WILLIAM AND MARY BUREAU

Teardrop draw pull *Precursor to Victorian style, but much heavier*

Ball foot

Serpentine stretcher

QUEEN ANNE

Spanning most of the first half of the 18th Century, the Queen Anne style was both influential and original, its furniture characterized by refined, flowing lines with minimal decoration. The style spawned an important innovation in furniture making: the cabriole leg. Queen Anne designs migrated to the Colonies well after being established in England, eventually finding a home in Philadelphia, America's most important cabinetmaking center.

QUEEN ANNE CHAIR

TALL CHEST

Curved chair back

Padded slip seat

Large brass back plate with bail

Cabriole leg

CHIPPENDALE

Named after British carver and furniture designer Thomas Chippendale, the style that bears his name emerged in the second half of the 18th Century. It is often thought of as Queen Anne dressed up with ornamentation such as shell carvings, intricate fretwork, piecrust edging, and other elements of rococo or Chinese design.

HIGHBOY

Broken pediment crown molding

TEA TABLE

Rococo carvings

Rosette pull

Cabriole leg

Claw-and-ball foot

BLOCK-FRONT DESK
An American adaption of the Chippendale style

Shell carving

Built in Philadelphia in the 1770s, this chair is a good example of Chippendale's rococo style. It is closer to British design than the more indigenous styles being made at the same time in the other major furniture making centers of America.

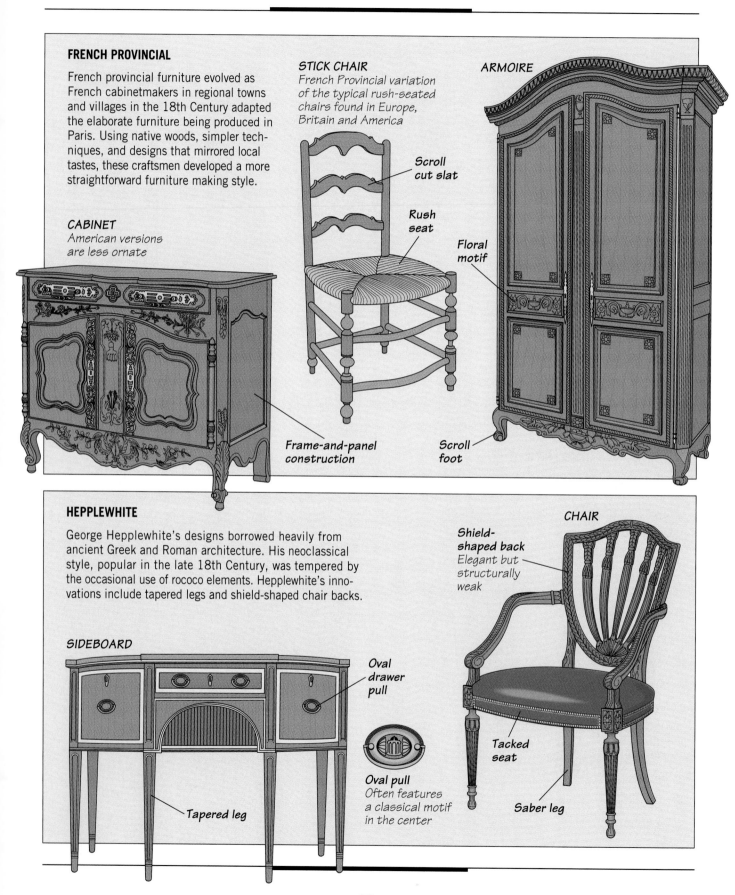

FRENCH PROVINCIAL

French provincial furniture evolved as French cabinetmakers in regional towns and villages in the 18th Century adapted the elaborate furniture being produced in Paris. Using native woods, simpler techniques, and designs that mirrored local tastes, these craftsmen developed a more straightforward furniture making style.

CABINET
American versions are less ornate

STICK CHAIR
French Provincial variation of the typical rush-seated chairs found in Europe, Britain and America

Scroll cut slat

Rush seat

Frame-and-panel construction

ARMOIRE

Floral motif

Scroll foot

HEPPLEWHITE

George Hepplewhite's designs borrowed heavily from ancient Greek and Roman architecture. His neoclassical style, popular in the late 18th Century, was tempered by the occasional use of rococo elements. Hepplewhite's innovations include tapered legs and shield-shaped chair backs.

SIDEBOARD

Tapered leg

Oval drawer pull

Oval pull
Often features a classical motif in the center

CHAIR

Shield-shaped back
Elegant but structurally weak

Tacked seat

Saber leg

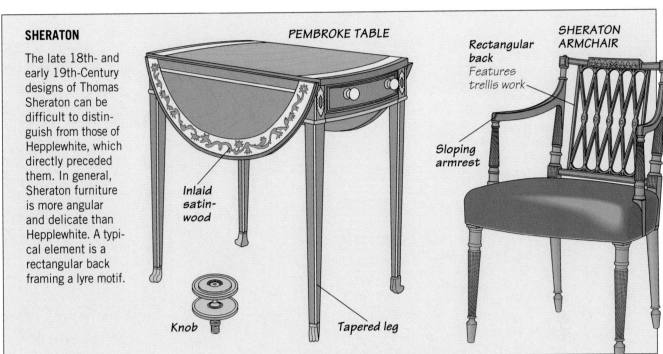

SHERATON

The late 18th- and early 19th-Century designs of Thomas Sheraton can be difficult to distinguish from those of Hepplewhite, which directly preceded them. In general, Sheraton furniture is more angular and delicate than Hepplewhite. A typical element is a rectangular back framing a lyre motif.

PEMBROKE TABLE

Inlaid satin-wood

Knob

Tapered leg

SHERATON ARMCHAIR

Rectangular back
Features trellis work

Sloping armrest

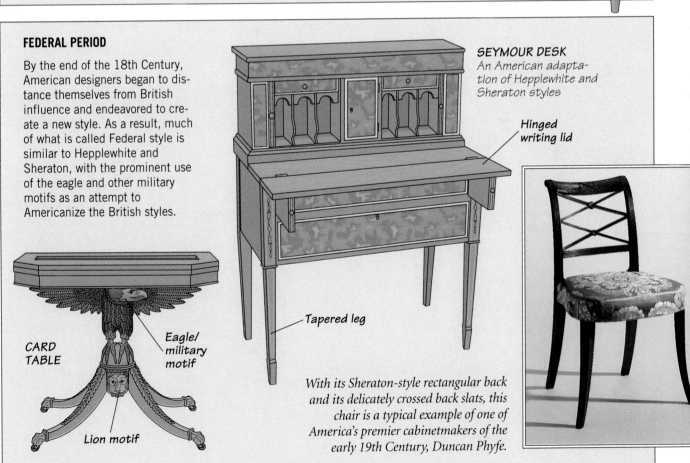

FEDERAL PERIOD

By the end of the 18th Century, American designers began to distance themselves from British influence and endeavored to create a new style. As a result, much of what is called Federal style is similar to Hepplewhite and Sheraton, with the prominent use of the eagle and other military motifs as an attempt to Americanize the British styles.

SEYMOUR DESK
An American adaptation of Hepplewhite and Sheraton styles

Hinged writing lid

CARD TABLE

Eagle/ military motif

Lion motif

Tapered leg

With its Sheraton-style rectangular back and its delicately crossed back slats, this chair is a typical example of one of America's premier cabinetmakers of the early 19th Century, Duncan Phyfe.

SHAKER

The Shakers were a puritanical religious sect that prospered in the 1800s, mainly in New England and New York State. They lived in isolation from society on self-sufficient communal farms. Shaker furniture faithfully reflects their belief that usefulness is the highest good. Their pieces are practical, functional, and austere—without extravagance or ornamentation—but attractive in their simplicity. Shaker design principles continue to inspire modern furniture makers.

The beauty of Shaker furniture lies in its clean lines and complete devotion to function. Candle stands, like the one shown at left, had either round, square, or rectangular tops. Oval or octagonal shapes were considered frivolous and therefore too flashy.

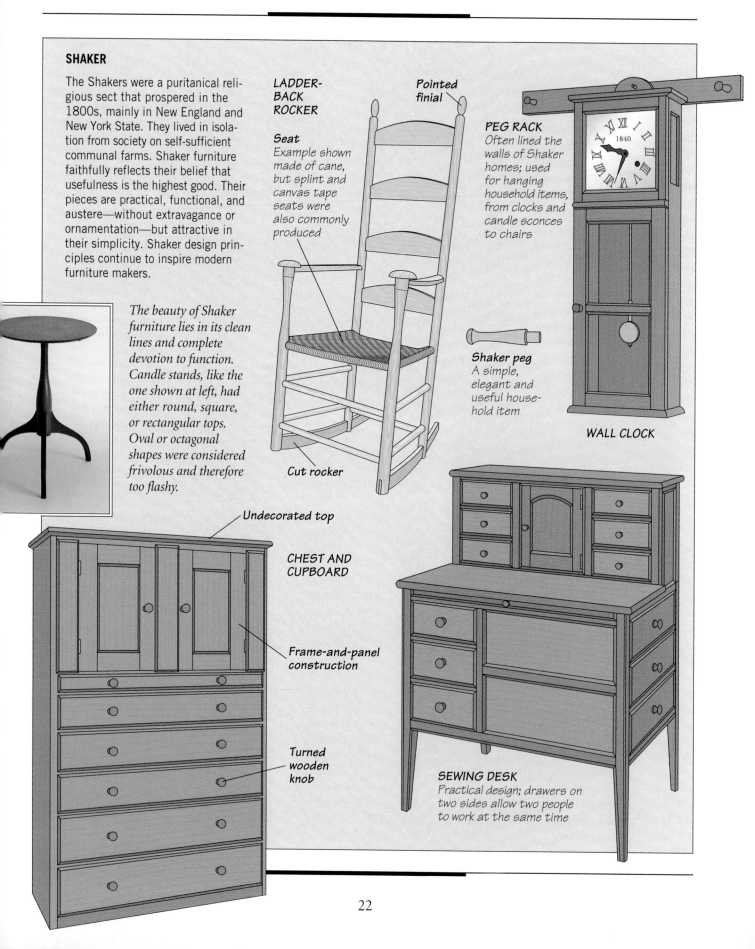

LADDER-BACK ROCKER

Pointed finial

Seat
Example shown made of cane, but splint and canvas tape seats were also commonly produced

Cut rocker

PEG RACK
Often lined the walls of Shaker homes; used for hanging household items, from clocks and candle sconces to chairs

Shaker peg
A simple, elegant and useful household item

WALL CLOCK

Undecorated top

CHEST AND CUPBOARD

Frame-and-panel construction

Turned wooden knob

SEWING DESK
Practical design: drawers on two sides allow two people to work at the same time

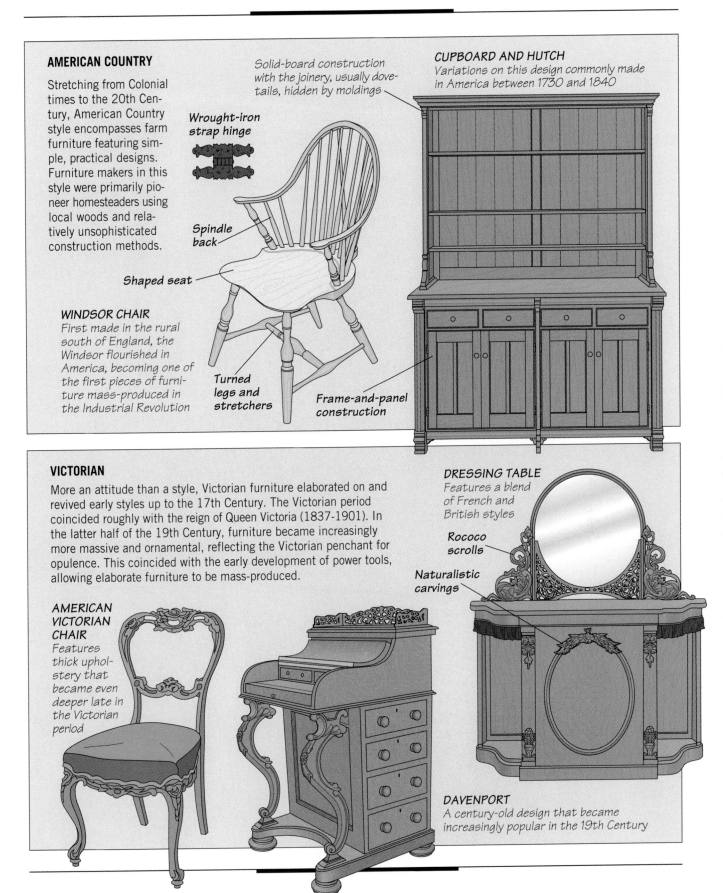

AMERICAN COUNTRY

Stretching from Colonial times to the 20th Century, American Country style encompasses farm furniture featuring simple, practical designs. Furniture makers in this style were primarily pioneer homesteaders using local woods and relatively unsophisticated construction methods.

Wrought-iron strap hinge

Solid-board construction with the joinery, usually dovetails, hidden by moldings

Spindle back

Shaped seat

WINDSOR CHAIR

First made in the rural south of England, the Windsor flourished in America, becoming one of the first pieces of furniture mass-produced in the Industrial Revolution

Turned legs and stretchers

Frame-and-panel construction

CUPBOARD AND HUTCH

Variations on this design commonly made in America between 1730 and 1840

VICTORIAN

More an attitude than a style, Victorian furniture elaborated on and revived early styles up to the 17th Century. The Victorian period coincided roughly with the reign of Queen Victoria (1837-1901). In the latter half of the 19th Century, furniture became increasingly more massive and ornamental, reflecting the Victorian penchant for opulence. This coincided with the early development of power tools, allowing elaborate furniture to be mass-produced.

AMERICAN VICTORIAN CHAIR

Features thick upholstery that became even deeper late in the Victorian period

DRESSING TABLE

Features a blend of French and British styles

Rococo scrolls

Naturalistic carvings

DAVENPORT

A century-old design that became increasingly popular in the 19th Century

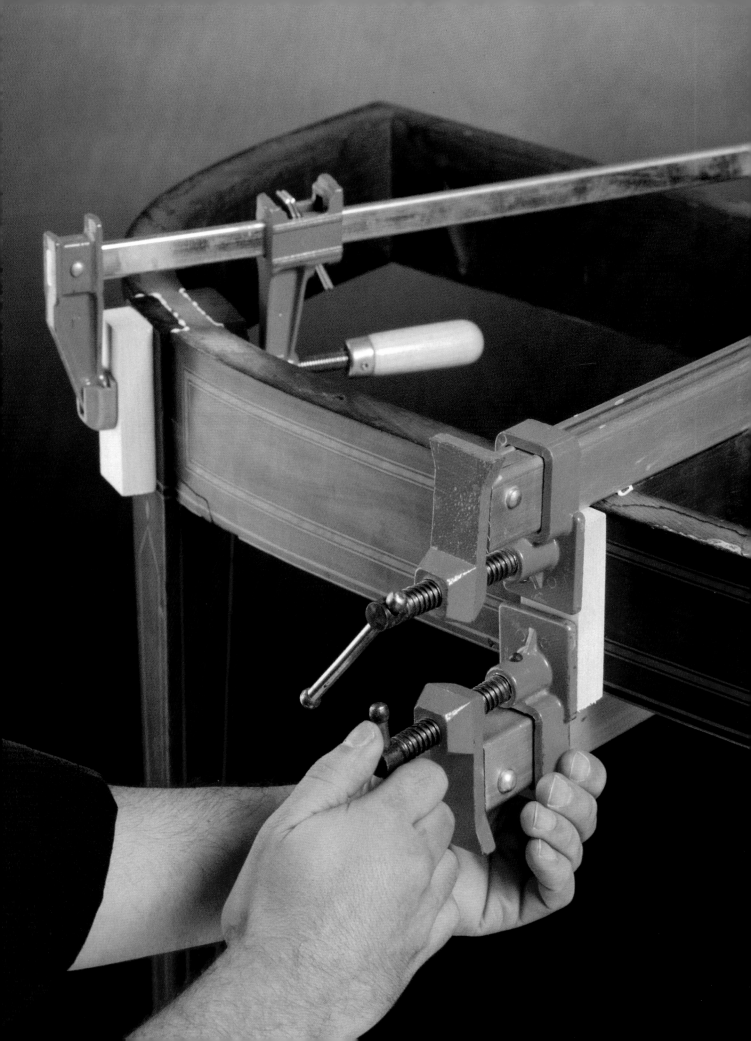

REPAIRING JOINTS

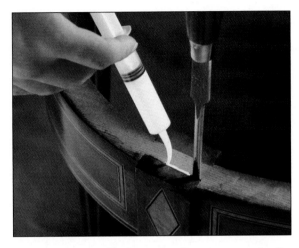

Joints in antique furniture often loosen as a result of a deterioration of the glue bond. When it is impossible or unnecessary to disassemble a joint, as in the bridle joint in the table shown above, you can use a flat-tip screwdriver to gently pry it open. This will enable you to clean out the joint and apply fresh adhesive, using a syringe-type glue injector. The joint can then be clamped, as shown in the photo on page 24.

Restoring antique furniture can be approached in much the same way that hospital emergency rooms tackle medical crises. Doctors handle a flood of patients using a process called triage: Life-threatening emergencies are cared for first, followed by problems of lesser gravity. Applied to furniture repair, this triage process means that broken, loose, and wobbly joints should be your first concern. Other problems, such as surface damage and blemishes, or finishes that need to be repaired or stripped and redone, can wait until all the joinery is sound and sturdy.

The first step in restoring any piece of furniture is to develop a plan of action. As discussed on page 26, start with a careful inspection of the piece and note all the problems that need to be remedied. You can then devise a strategy for making the repairs.

This chapter presents a collection of proven techniques for fixing and strengthening the joints most commonly found in antiques. In most cases, loose or damaged joints must be disassembled before they can be repaired. Starting on page 27 are various methods for breaking the glue bond that holds joints together. Techniques for extracting the nails and screws used to reinforce joints in some antiques are also described *(page 29)*. Once disassembled, the joint can be cleaned thoroughly and re-glued.

Classic joints like the mortise-and-tenon and dovetail have been used to assemble good-quality furniture for centuries. The chapter will also explain how to repair often-encountered variations of these joints, including round mortise-and-tenons *(page 32)* and through dovetails *(page 34)*.

Two loose joints on the card table shown at left are being reglued and clamped together. A single bar clamp secures an open mortise-and-tenon joint connecting a leg to the apron. Two clamps hold a sliding dovetail between the apron and a rail. In both cases, the joints were cleaned out and glue was injected between the mating surfaces. Wood pads protect the stock and help distribute the clamping pressure.

REPAIR STRATEGY

The first step in restoring an antique piece of furniture is to inspect it carefully and list all the damaged parts in need of repair. As a graphic aid, you can make a rough sketch of the piece and highlight the areas of damage. The illustrations of the desk and table below show the types of problems you are likely to find, and indicate the pages in this and the following chapters that include step-by-step repair instructions. Examine all external surfaces, including the back and bottom. Look for split panels, loose joinery, cracked veneer, stains in the finish, and other defects. Check any parts that are movable, such as tilting tops, or removable, such as drawers. Try to assess the impact that a defect could have on the overall structure of the piece. A chair leg that is shorter than the others, for example, is quite serious, for the resulting imbalance could stress and weaken all of the leg-to-rail joints, or cause the seat to crack.

Next, decide how to make each repair. A loose joint, for example, can sometimes be fixed by prying it open slightly and injecting glue into the seam, as shown in the color photo on page 25. However, if excessive pressure is applied, you may weaken or even break the other joints in the piece, causing even greater damage to the piece.

In such cases, you are better disassembling the piece and cleaning out and regluing all of the joints at once.

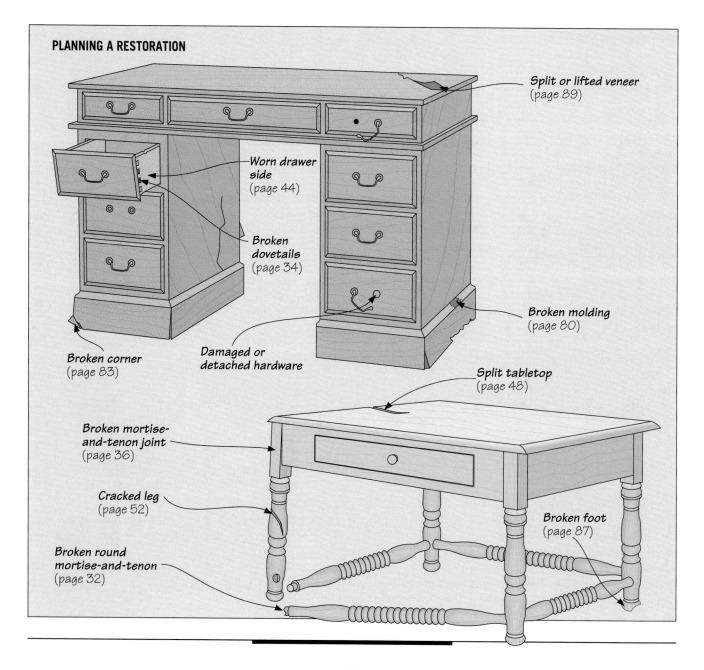

PLANNING A RESTORATION

Split or lifted veneer (page 89)

Worn drawer side (page 44)

Broken dovetails (page 34)

Broken corner (page 83)

Damaged or detached hardware

Broken molding (page 80)

Split tabletop (page 48)

Broken mortise-and-tenon joint (page 36)

Cracked leg (page 52)

Broken foot (page 87)

Broken round mortise-and-tenon (page 32)

DISASSEMBLING FURNITURE

Many repairs to the joinery of an antique will involve taking some or all of the joints apart. Start by determining how the joints are secured together. If only glue was used, all you need to do is break the glue bond. Begin with methods that are least likely to damage the piece. Since many antique pieces were assembled with animal hide glues, exposing the adhesive to steam, as shown below, may do the trick. With modern glues, methyl alcohol often proves effective. As a last resort, use clamping pressure to spread the joints *(page 28)*.

You may have to repair a piece assembled with fasteners, such as nails, screws, or wooden pegs. Beginning on page 29 are several techniques for extracting fasteners from a piece of furniture.

Normally thought of as a carpentry tool, a pry bar like the one shown at right can be indispensable in furniture restoration. Here, the bar is being used to pull a nail securing the leg of an armoire to its rail assembly. The wood pad increases leverage and protects the wood surface.

LOOSENING JOINTS

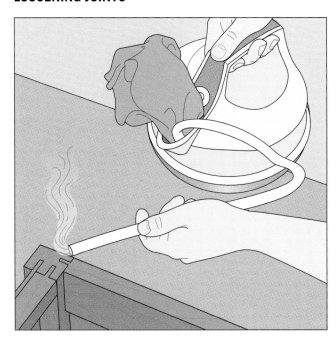

Using steam
Animal hide glue was commonly used by furniture makers of the past. Its major weakness—the tendency of the glue to soften when exposed to moisture or heat—is actually an advantage for furniture restorers. To disassemble a joint that may have been secured with hide glue, apply steam to it. For a cabinet like the one shown above, remove the top to expose as many of the joints as possible. Then attach a rubber hose to an electric kettle, stuff the spout with a rag to force the steam out through the hose, and plug it in. Once steam begins to come out of the hose, hold the end against the joint for a few minutes. Repeat for the other joints, then pull them apart using hand pressure, a mallet, or clamps *(page 28)*.

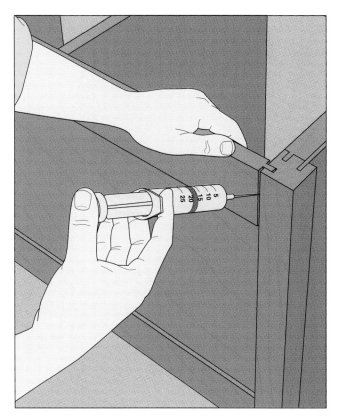

Injecting methyl alcohol
If steam fails to break the glue bonds, the joints may have been glued up with a modern chemical-based adhesive. In this case, load a syringe with methyl alcohol and inject a bead along each glue line *(above)*. Avoid spreading the liquid beyond the glue line, since methyl alcohol can damage finishes. Let the methylated spirits soak into the joints for a few minutes, then take them apart.

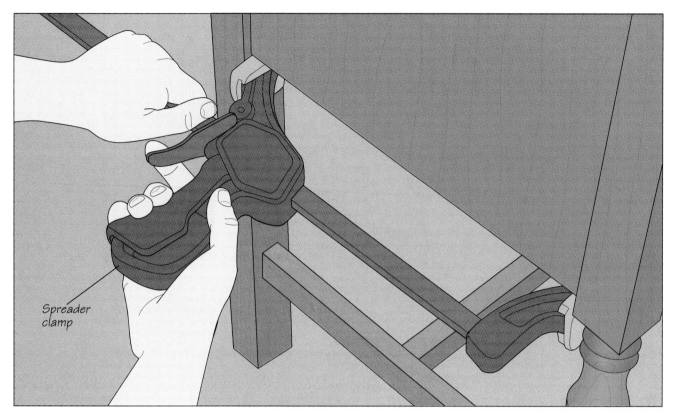

Spreader clamp

Prying joints apart

Although clamps are usually made to press joints together, some can also be used to spread them apart. To separate the legs from a carcase, as shown above, install a spreader clamp between each pair of front and back legs, positioning the jaws as close to the joints as possible. Tighten each clamp gradually, spreading the legs apart, until you feel some resistance. Then tap the legs sharply with a dead blow hammer, loosening the joints further. Continue, tightening the clamps and tapping the legs apart until the joint separates and you can free the legs from the piece. (You can also use some types of bar clamps to perform the same work as a spreader clamp by reversing the heads on the clamps.)

SHOP TIP

Prying off the back of a cabinet
To remove the back from a cabinet, use wooden wedges. Starting at one corner, insert a wedge into the joint between the back and the sides and tap the piece of wood with a mallet. Repeat at 4- to 6-inch intervals until enough of the back has lifted to enable you to pry it off without damaging it. The same technique can also be used to pry a tabletop off the rails that hold it in place.

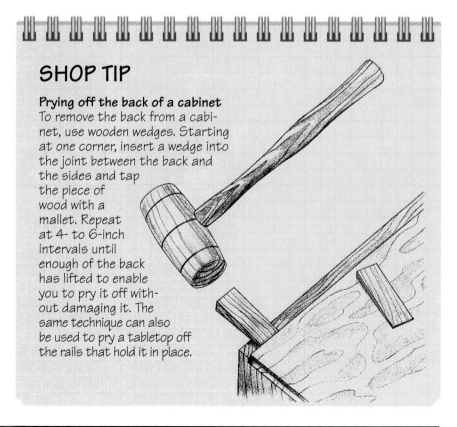

EXTRACTING FASTENERS

Loosening a nail

It is not uncommon to find that a joint that has failed in the past has received a quick fix with the help of a few nails. One method for loosening a nail that is snug and flush with the surface of the wood or countersunk below it is to hold the tip of a nail punch on the nail head and strike the punch with a hammer *(right)*. This often loosens the nail's grip in the wood. You can then pry out the head and remove the nail with pliers, as described below. Another technique involves using an old chisel to cut a small groove all around the nail head, working the tip of the blade under the head and prying it out enough so that you can grip the head with the pliers. Work carefully to avoid gouging the wood more than is necessary. A third technique is to use a soldering iron, as shown on page 30.

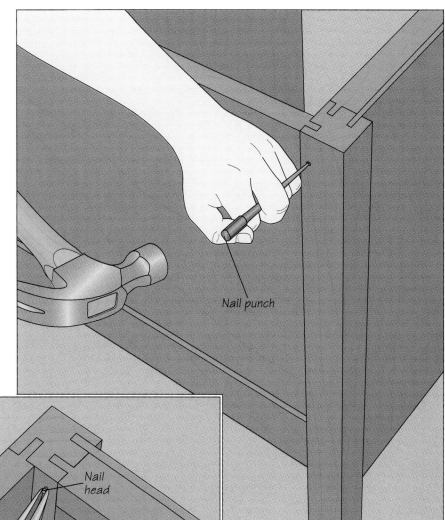

Nail punch

Nail head

Pulling a nail

To extract a loosened nail without damaging the surrounding wood, use needle-nose pliers *(left)*. Gripping the nail head in the jaws, use a combination of gentle twisting and pulling to work the nail out of its hole.

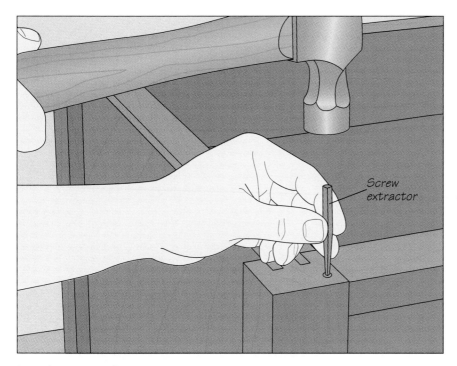

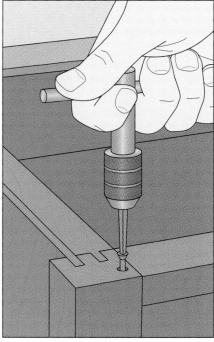

Removing a screw with an extractor

If the head of a screw is so damaged that you cannot remove the fastener with a screwdriver, try using a screw extractor. Start by fitting an electric drill with a twist bit slightly smaller than the tip of the extractor, then drill a shallow hole in the center of the screw head. Holding the tip of the extractor in the hole, strike it with a hammer a few times until the device is firmly anchored to the screw *(above, left)*. Attach the handle-and-chuck assembly to the extractor and then turn the handle counterclockwise to loosen and remove the screw *(above, right)*.

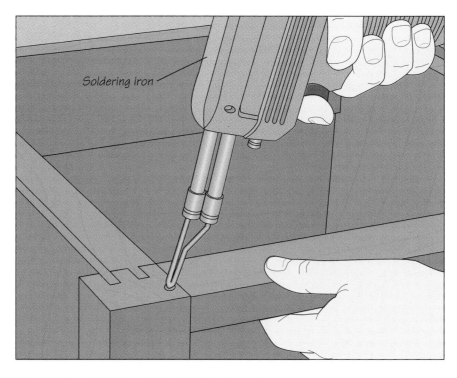

Loosening a fastener with a soldering iron

Metals expand when they are heated and contract when cooled. You can use this principle to your advantage to loosen a snug-fitting nail or screw. Install a fine tip on a soldering iron and allow it to heat up. Then hold the hot tip on the nail or screw head for a few minutes *(right)*. Work carefully to avoid burning the surrounding wood. The heat will be transferred along the length of the fastener, causing it to expand enough to enlarge its hole. Remove the soldering iron, let the fastener cool, and remove it.

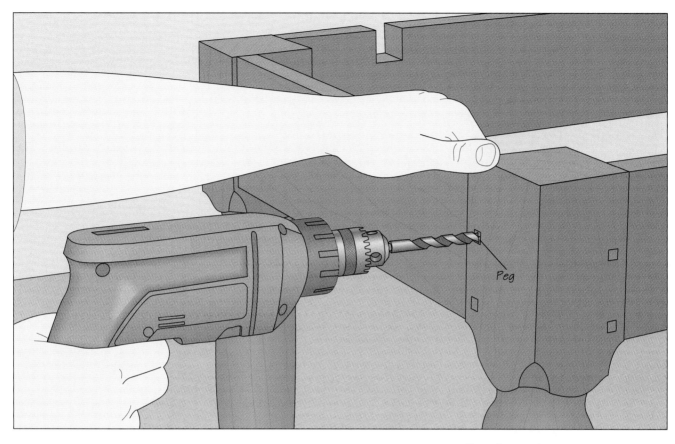

Peg

Removing wooden pegs

Joints are often reinforced with glued-in wooden pegs, as in the mortise-and-tenons shown above. To disassemble this joint, you need to first remove the pegs. Fit an electric drill with a bit that matches the size of the pegs as closely as possible. Then center the bit on one of the pegs and drill it out, boring your hole the entire length of the peg. Repeat for the remaining pegs, then dismantle the joint *(page 27)*.

SHOP TIP

Increasing the torque of a screwdriver

To remove a stubborn screw, tighten a pair of locking pliers (or a crescent wrench) around the shank of a screwdriver just below the handle, as shown at right. Then fit the tip of the screwdriver into the slot in the screw head. Pushing the screwdriver down with one hand and keeping it vertical, use the pliers as a handle to turn it.

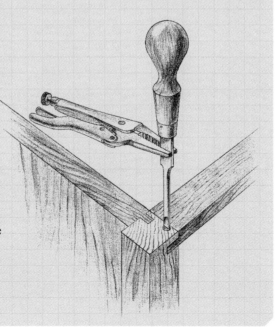

JOINERY REPAIRS

Most well-built antiques were assembled with classic, hand-crafted joints, such as mortise-and-tenons and dovetails. Although these joints are renowned for their strength, they cannot be expected to last forever.

There is usually more than one way to repair a loose or damaged joint, but your main concern is to make a durable repair. Sometimes, that can be accomplished by cleaning out the joint, injecting fresh adhesive, and clamping up the joint. At other times, such half-measures will not work or last.

The following pages show step-by-step repairs for a variety of typical problems you may encounter in repairing antique furniture joinery. The best solution for a mortise-and-tenon joint with a broken tenon, for example, is to replace the tenon with a dowel *(below)* or a spline *(page 36)*. A loose dovetail joint can be fixed by cutting a kerf between the affected pin and tail, and gluing in a strip of veneer. But a dovetail with a broken pin or tail must be taken apart so that the joint can be rebuilt *(page 34)*.

Three loose round mortise-and-tenon joints between the legs and stretchers of the table shown at left are being glued back together. Each joint was tightened by kerfing the tenon and inserting a wedge into the cut. One bar clamp secures a stretcher to the front and back legs, and another holds two stretchers together. Woods pads are used to protect the stock; one of the pads was arched to conform to the contours of the stretcher.

REPAIRING A BROKEN ROUND TENON

1 Cutting off the tenon
To repair a round mortise-and-tenon joint with a broken tenon, cut away the tenon; it will be replaced by a dowel *(step 3)*. Secure the workpiece in a bench vise and use a backsaw to cut off the tenon flush with the shoulder *(right)*. Hold the saw perfectly parallel to the shoulder throughout the cut.

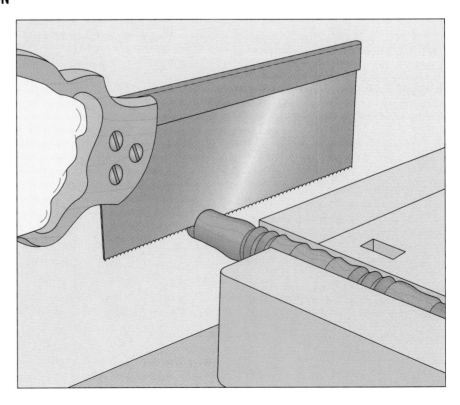

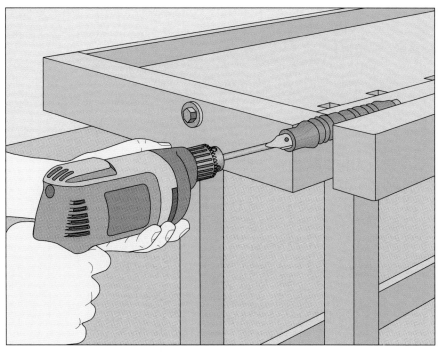

2 Preparing the workpiece for a dowel

Install a drill bit the same diameter as the original tenon. Then with the workpiece still secured in the vise, center the tip of the bit on the cut end of the workpiece. Holding the drill level, bore a hole to the same depth as the tenon you cut off *(above)*.

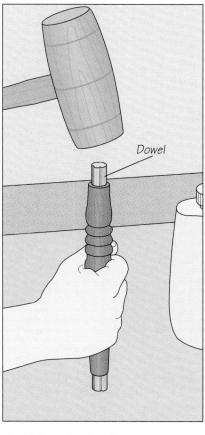

Dowel

3 Gluing in the dowel

Secure a length of dowel the same diameter as the original tenon in the vise and cut a piece twice as long as the depth of the hole you drilled in step 2. To permit excess glue to escape from the hole when you install the dowel, use a chisel to cut a few shallow grooves along the length of the dowel. Then spread glue on the dowel and insert it in the hole in your workpiece. Tap the dowel with a mallet until it is fully seated in its hole *(above)*. Once the glue has cured, glue up the original joint. A typical clamping arrangement for round mortise-and-tenons is shown in the color photo on page 32.

SHOP TIP

Sizing up a dowel
Over time, the mortise housing a round tenon can enlarge, loosening the joint. One solution is to wrap a strip of cloth around the tenon to increase its diameter. Cut the cloth as wide as the length of the tenon, coat it with glue and wrap it around the tenon, as shown at right. Spread glue in the mortise and clamp the joint.

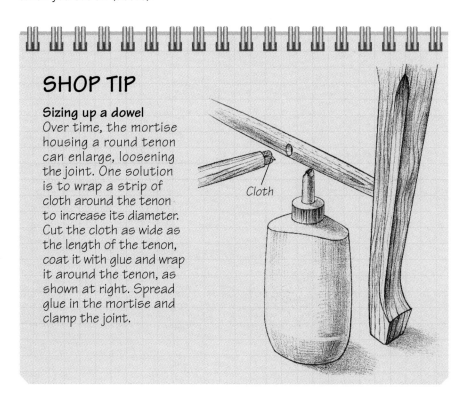

Cloth

REPAIRING A LOOSE DOVETAIL

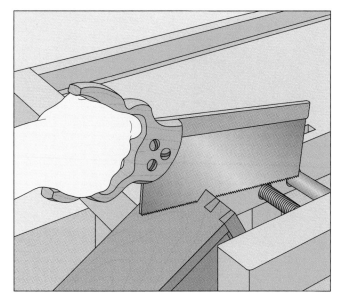

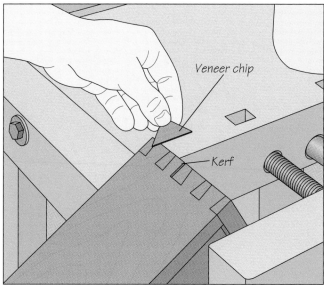

Gluing in a veneer strip

Dovetail joints are renowned for their strength and durability. But even these sturdy joints can eventually work loose—the result of years of wood contraction and swelling due to humidity changes, or deterioration of the glue bond. To fill a small gap between a pin and tail, use a thin triangle of veneer. For the drawer shown above, secure the workpiece in a bench vise so the loose joint is facing up and use a backsaw to straighten

out or deepen the gap to the joint's shoulder line *(above, left)*. Then, cut a triangular piece of veneer to fit into the kerf. To make the chip less obvious, choose veneer that matches the workpiece as closely as possible and cut it so that its grain will run diagonally in the joint. Apply a little glue in the kerf and insert the traingle *(above, right)*. Once the adhesive has cured, use a chisel to trim the veneer flush with the surface.

REPLACING A BROKEN DOVETAIL

1 Outlining the damaged tails
To repair damaged dovetails, cut them out and replace them, following the steps shown here and on page 35. To prepare the workpiece, such as the drawer shown at right, set it on a work surface with the damaged tails facing up. Then align a straightedge with one side of the tail and use a pencil to mark a cutting line on the surface from the top end of the tail to a point a few inches below it. Repeat on the other side of the tail, making sure the two lines intersect. Outline any other damaged tails the same way. Once all the cutting lines have been marked, carefully disassemble the joints.

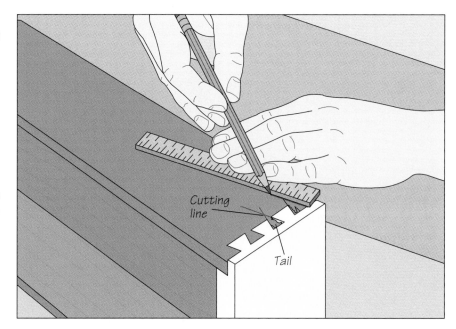

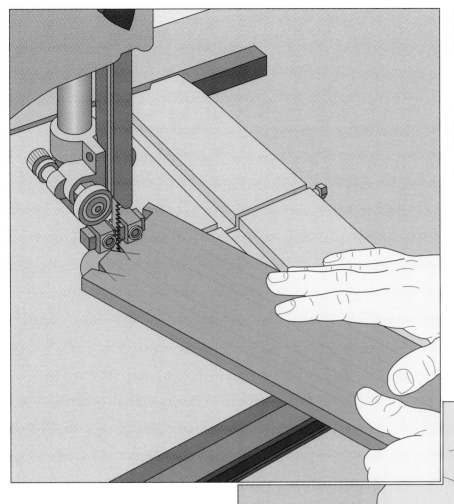

2 Cutting out the damaged tails

Cut out the broken tails on your band saw. Holding the tail board flat on the machine table, feed the board into the blade to saw along one of your cutting lines. Stop the cut at the apex of the V formed by the two marks outlining the same tail. Repeat for the second mark to sever the tail, forming a wedge-shaped gap in the end of the board. Saw off the other damaged tails the same way *(left)*.

Replacement tail

3 Making and gluing in the replacement tails

Make the replacement tails from a board the same thickness as the workpiece and one that matches it as closely as possible. (In the illustration at right, the tails are shown in a lighter shade for visual clarity.) Outline as many tails as you need on the board, using an undamaged tail from the workpiece as a template. Remember to extend each outline to include the triangular wedge below the tails. Cut the tails out on the band saw, spread glue on the edges of each one, and fit them into the gaps you cut in the workpiece. Once the glue has cured, glue up the joint.

REPAIRING A BROKEN BLIND MORTISE-AND-TENON

1 Cleaning glue residue from the mortise
A blind mortise-and-tenon joint with a damaged tenon is repaired in much the same way as a broken round mortise-and-tenon *(page 32)*. In this case, the tenon is removed and replaced with a spline *(step 3)*. Start by disassembling the joint and clamping the mortise piece—in this example, a leg—to a work surface so the mortise is facing up. Chisel out any pieces of the broken tenon and any glue residue, making sure the sides of the mortise are straight and even. Finish the job with a lock mortise chisel, cleaning and flattening the bottom of the mortise *(right)*.

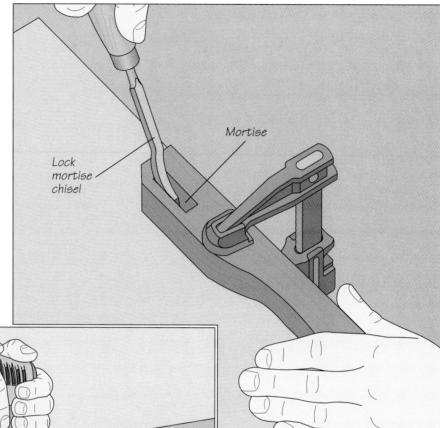

Lock mortise chisel

Mortise

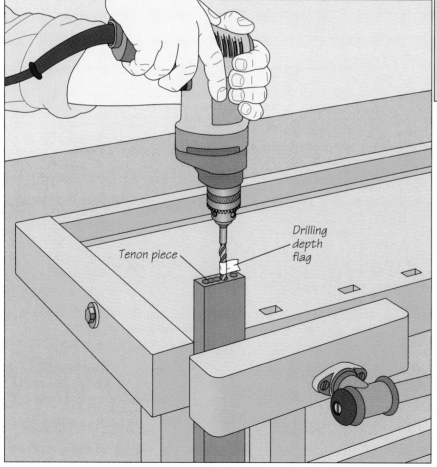

Tenon piece

Drilling depth flag

2 Preparing the tenon piece for a spline
Cut off the tenon flush with the shoulder; follow the same procedure you would use for a round tenon *(page 32)*. Secure the piece upright in a bench vise, then fit an electric drill with a bit the same diameter as the mortise width. Fasten a strip of tape to the bit to mark the drilling depth—equal to the depth of the mortise. Starting at one end of the tenon, center the bit on the surface of the workpiece—in this case, a rail—and bore a hole; stop when the drilling depth flag contacts the surface. Continue *(left)*, drilling a row of overlapping holes until you reach the other end of the tenon. To finish the mortise, use a chisel to even out the sides and bottom of the cavity.

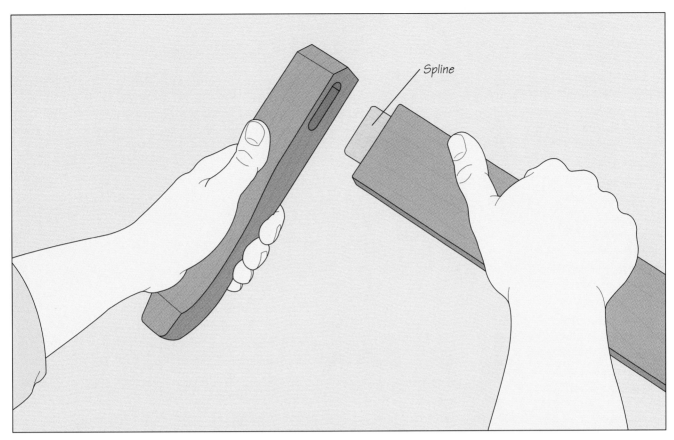

Spline

3 Gluing up the joint

To join the leg and rail together, cut a spline to fit snugly in the mortises; make its length slightly less than the combined depth of the two mortises. Spread glue on the spline, insert it into one of the mortises and tap it in all the way with a mallet. Then fit the other mortise over the exposed end of the spline *(above)* and use a clamp to secure the joint.

SHOP TIP

Wedging a loose through tenon
You can tighten up a loose-fitting through mortise-and-tenon without taking the joint apart. Use a wooden mallet and chisel the same width as the tenon thickness to cut two kerfs into the end of the tenon, one near each edge. Make the cuts 1 or 2 inches deep into the stock. Then cut two wedges as wide as the chisel blade, coat them with glue, and drive them into the kerfs, as shown at right. Trim the wedges flush with the end of the tenon.

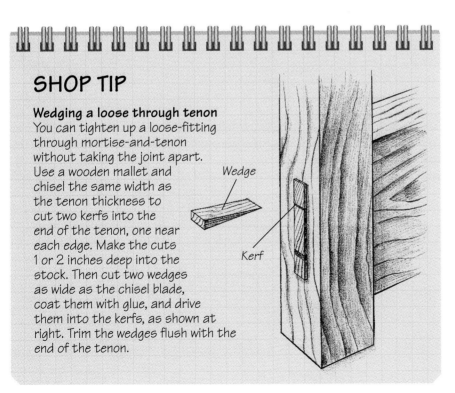

Wedge

Kerf

MAJOR REPAIRS

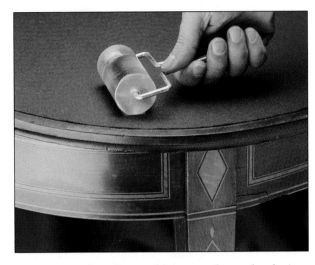

A covering of wool/rayon felt is pressed onto the playing surface of the gateleg card table shown above, rejuvenating the worn tabletop. Once a layer of fabric glue is spread on the surface, the felt is set in position and smoothed into place with a veneer roller.

The average woodworker may readily strip and refinish a piece of antique furniture or fill in a gouged wood surface, but many balk at undertaking more involved fixes, such as flattening a cupped top, straightening a warped door, or mending a split chair seat. And yet these are precisely the types of repairs that can restore an affordable flea-market bargain to its rightful status as a beautiful, usable antique.

The following pages describe how to repair major faults typically found in antique casework, drawers, tables, and chairs. There is nothing mysterious about the process; what makes these fixes challenging is that they must go beyond restoring a piece's original appearance by shoring up the furniture's structural strength.

Repairs to furniture that simply satisfy appearances are often too weak to survive regular use. These need extra bracing which must be concealed. A broken turned leg *(page 52)* is easy enough to glue and clamp together, but the resulting joint cannot be trusted. The answer is to insert a dowel to reinforce the repair. Another example is a split chair seat. Once the seat is glued together, butterfly keys *(page 58)* are added to strengthen the glue bond, as shown in the photo on page 38.

Repairing a cupped tabletop involves more than simply flattening the surface. As shown beginning on page 46, you need to repair this flaw without weakening the table. To take another example, a split bent-wood chair back is not merely a surface defect, but a fault that weakens the structural integrity of the piece. By resteaming the wood *(page 56)*, you can repair the problem and recover much of the original strength of the bend.

Of all the components of furniture, chair seats typically face the most abuse. Pages 61 to 73 detail methods for redoing cane, rush, and upholstered seats.

This chapter will show you step-by-step procedures for resurrecting many of these neglected treasures, proving that in many cases someone else's write-off often deserves a second look.

The seat of the antique chair shown at left, split by years of use, is being glued back together. With the addition of dovetailed butterfly keys on the seat's underside to reinforce the joint, the repair can be made inconspicuous and structurally sound.

Doors are the public face of most casework; like most faces, they are often asked to accomplish the impossible. Although they are hinged on only one side, they must swing freely, hang straight and level, and rest flat against the cabinet front. Inevitably, the doors of many older pieces are often twisted, loose, and damaged.

Twisted frame-and-panel doors are usually the result of a warped stile—one of the vertical frame pieces of the door. Sometimes, the only solution is to replace the stile. But because this option can destroy the authenticity of the piece, you should first try to straighten the stile, as shown below.

After years of swinging open and being slammed shut, most doors eventually start to sag on their hinges. Often, the screws have worn away the wood, leaving holes that are larger than the screw threads. Refer to page 42 for making an invisible repair to correct this fault.

The panel of a correctly made frame-and-panel door is never glued into the frame. This is to allow the panel to expand and contract with humidity changes. There is an added advantage for the furniture restorer. A split panel can be mended simply by drawing the two pieces together without disassembling the frame. This is shown on page 43.

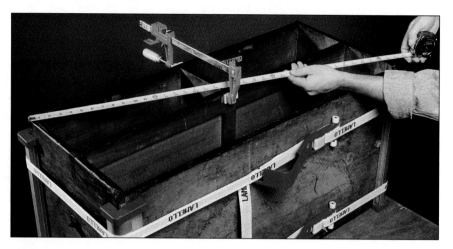

Clamping the corners of a large carcase like the 18th-Century captain's chest shown above presents special problems. To apply adequate pressure without twisting the joints out-of-square, a pair of web clamps are used, one at the bottom and another at the top. Corner brackets distribute the pressure along the joints and a single bar clamp secures the divider in place. You can check for square by measuring the diagonals between opposite corners. The carcase is square if the two results are the same. If not, place a clamp across the longer of the two diagonals and tighten, then recheck your measurements.

REPAIRING A TWISTED FRAME-AND-PANEL DOOR

1 Cutting kerfs in the stile
A warped frame-and-panel door usually has a warped stile—one of the vertical frame members that house the panel. You should first try steaming the stile, using the technique shown on page 56, and then clamping the workpiece flat. If the warp is too severe, your only recourse is to kerf the stile. Clamp the piece outside-face down to a work surface, then use a try square to mark a series of lines about 1/2 inch apart across the face of the stile where it is curved. Use a backsaw to cut kerfs, using the lines as guides. The cuts should be about one-third to one-half as deep as the stock's thickness.

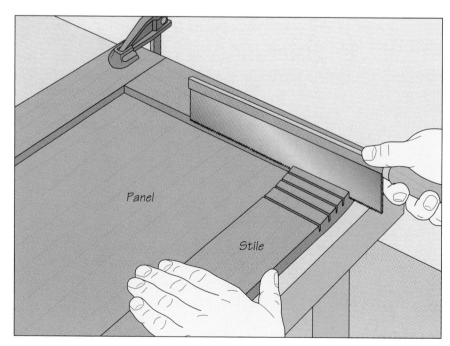

Panel

Stile

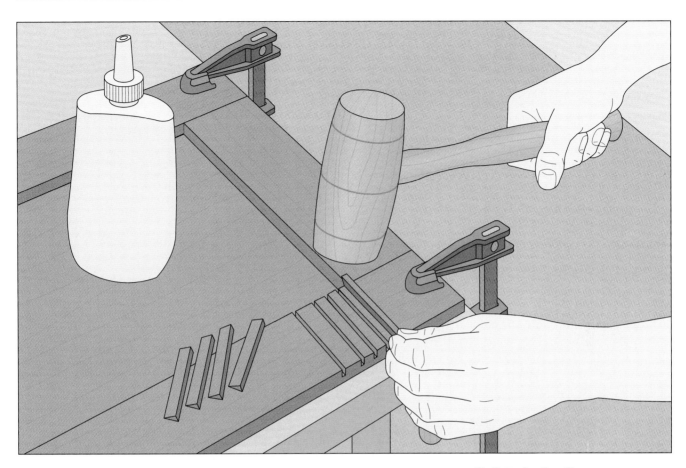

2 Flattening the stile
Once the kerfs are cut, flatten the warped stile by clamping it down to the work surface at each end. To keep the stile permanently flat, cut triangular-shaped wedges from a matching wood to fill the kerfs. Spread glue on the wedges and in the kerfs and use a wooden mallet to tap each one in place *(above)*.

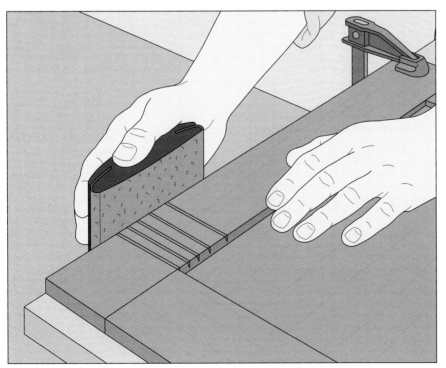

3 Finishing the repair
Once the glue has cured, use a chisel to trim the wedges flush with the edges and face of the stile. Then use a sanding block with fine sandpaper to smooth the area *(left)*. Identify the type of finish on the door *(page 96)*, then apply a matching finish to the surfaces that you sanded.

TIGHTENING LOOSE HINGES

1 Filling in the screw holes
Door hinges often work themselves loose when the screws fixing them in place enlarge their anchoring holes through repeated use and abuse. Set the piece on a work surface with the hinge facing up and remove the hinges from the carcase. Then, cut a length of dowel and taper its end to fit snugly into the screw holes of any loose hinge. For each screw hole, insert the dowel as far as it will go, mark a line on it flush with the surface of the carcase, withdraw the pin *(right)*, and trim it to length. Once all the dowels have been cut, spread glue on each one and tap it into its hole. Trim the dowels flush with the surface.

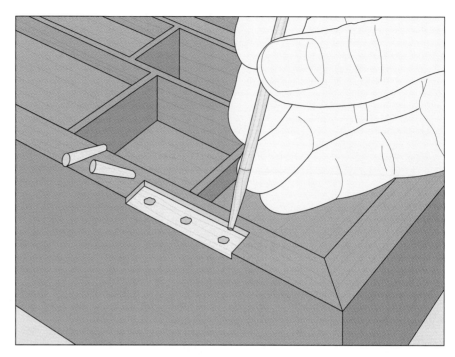

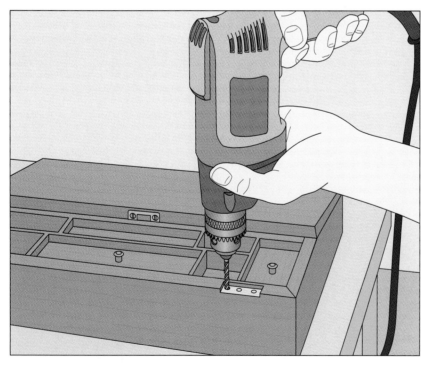

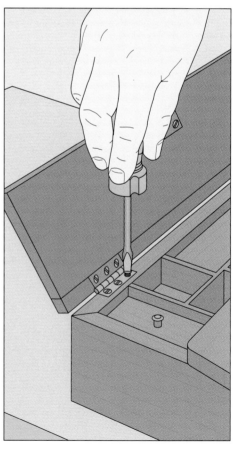

2 Mounting the hinge
Once the glue has cured, position the door and hinges on the carcase and mark screw holes where you inserted dowels. Then bore a pilot hole for each screw *(above)*. Reposition the door on the carcase and screw the hinges back in place *(right)*.

REPAIRING A SPLIT PANEL

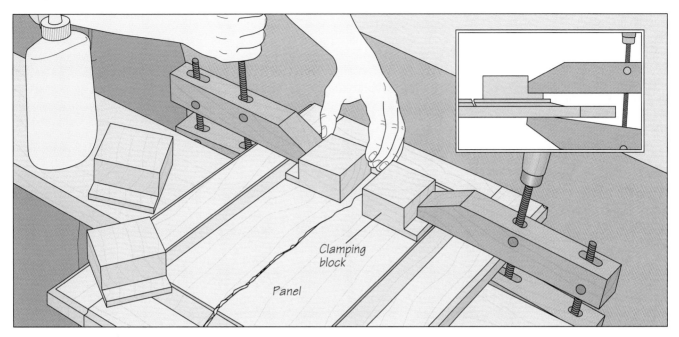

1 Preparing the panel

A split "floating" panel—one that is not glued into its frame—can be repaired easily. Because the edges and ends of the panel are free to move, the split seam can be drawn together without disassembling the frame. Set the workpiece right-side up on a work surface and prepare four clamping blocks for the panel. Cut a rabbet along an edge of each block, forming a lip. Then use a handscrew to clamp a pair of blocks to each end of the panel, placing the clamp jaw on the lip and aligning the lip along the edge of the adjacent stile *(above)*. The blocks should be long enough to accommodate a C clamp jaw *(step 2)* and thick enough to keep the handscrews from contacting the door stiles.

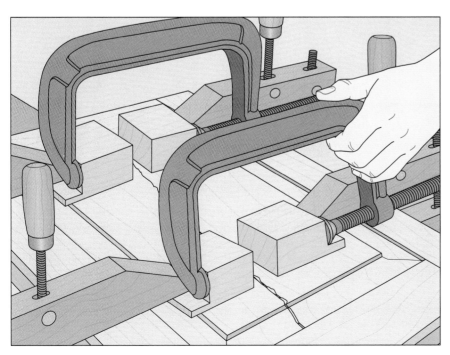

2 Gluing the panel

Spread glue in the crack in the panel, using a piece of stiff paper to work adhesive into any tight spots. Then install a C clamp on each pair of facing blocks, tightening the clamp to pull the blocks—and the split—together *(left)*. Keep tightening until the split is closed, making sure the handcrews are tight enough to prevent the blocks from slipping. Wipe off any glue squeeze-out with a damp cloth.

DRAWER REPAIRS

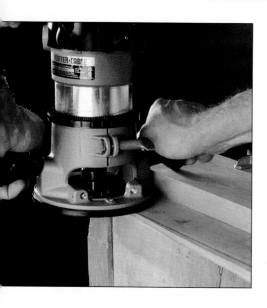

Drawers take as much abuse as any part of a piece of furniture. They are subjected to daily bouts of pulling, stuffing, and slamming. To counteract these stresses, well-built drawers are typically assembled with half-blind dovetails in front and through dovetails in back; both are strong and durable joints. Still, no joint will spare a drawer from worn sides or a split bottom—common signs of long years of wear and tear. This section describes fixes that will solve both problems.

Even dovetails are not impervious to damage, although they are one of the few joints that will hold together even if the glue fails. As shown on page 34 of the Repairing Joints chapter, these stalwart joints can be repaired and made as strong as new.

Guided by a straight board clamped to the drawer, a router levels the worn bottom edge of the drawer side shown at left. The cut is stopped short of the drawer front, leaving the tail end of the repair to a chisel. Together with split bottom panels, worn sides are the most common problem afflicting drawers in antique furniture.

REPAIRING WORN DRAWER SIDES

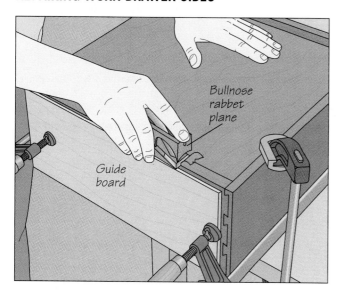

1 Leveling worn drawer sides
To level the bottom edge of a drawer side that is only slightly worn, build up the low spots by gluing down wood shims and sanding the surface flush. If the edges are badly worn, you can use a router *(photo, above)* or a bullnose rabbet plane to level the high spots. If you are using a plane, clamp the drawer to a work surface with the uneven edge facing up. Also clamp a guide board to the drawer side so the board's top edge is parallel with and slightly below the even part of the edge to be leveled. Unscrew the detachable nose of the plane to allow the blade to cut right up to the drawer front, then smooth the edge with even strokes *(above)* until the entire edge of the drawer side is level with the edge of the guide board.

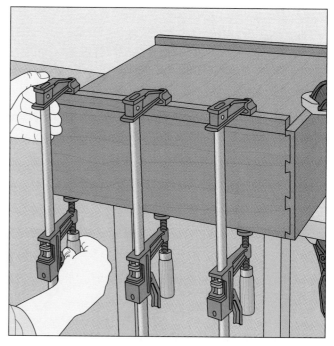

2 Rebuilding the drawer side
Once the edge of the drawer side is even, you need to restore the side to its original width. Select a piece of stock that matches the original color and grain pattern of the wood as closely as possible and cut it to the same length as the drawer sides. Also plane it to the same thickness and cut it a little wider than you will need to rebuild the drawer side. Spread glue on the contacting surfaces, remove the guide board and clamp the stock to the planed edge *(above)*.

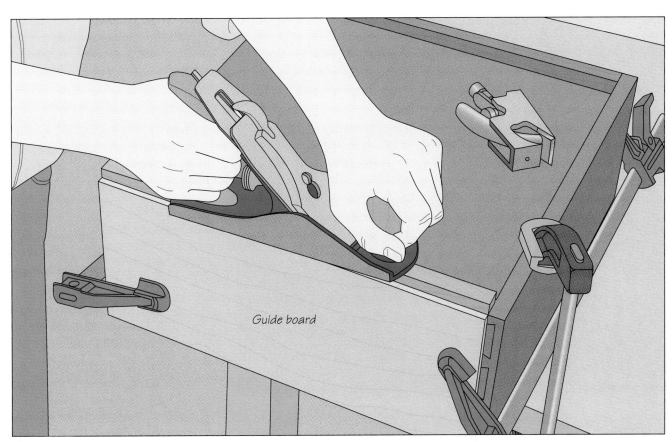

Guide board

3 Planing the drawer side to width
Once the glue has cured, secure the guide board to the drawer side once again, so its top edge is level with the top edge of the other drawer side. Starting with a bench plane *(above)*, cut the rebuilt drawer side down until it is almost level with the top edge of the guide board. Then, to avoid marring the drawer front, finish the job using the bullnose rabbet plane. Sand all surfaces of the rebuilt drawer side smooth.

SHOP TIP

Strengthening a split drawer bottom
A small split in a drawer bottom can be repaired with some glue and a piece of canvas. Set the drawer upside down on a work surface and clean the underside of the drawer bottom thoroughly. Then cut a piece of canvas to cover the split. Work some white glue or hide glue into the split and on the drawer bottom, then press the material into place, smoothing out any wrinkles.

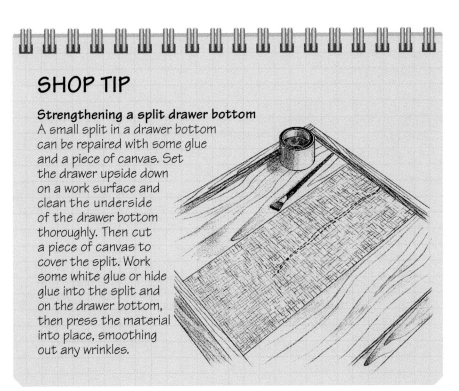

TABLE REPAIRS

Whether a tabletop is made from a single piece of lumber or from individual boards glued edge to edge, years of exposure to humidity levels that change from season to season can cause it to warp. Two effective remedies for cupped tabletops are shown below and on the following page.

Another frequent problem with tables is cracking or splitting of the top. Small cracks can be patched with strips of veneer, as described on page 48. With larger crevices, you need to be concerned with the structural integrity of the top as well as its appearance. To stop a split from becoming worse, you can install butterfly keys on the underside of the table *(page 58)*. Repairing the top of an inlaid leather desk calls for special techniques, as described starting on page 48.

A table's supporting structure—the leg-to-rail joinery—is also subject to the ravages of time and use. Repairs to common table joints, such as the mortise-and-tenon, are explained in the Repairing Joints chapter *(page 24)*. Fixing a damaged tripod table column is detailed on page 49.

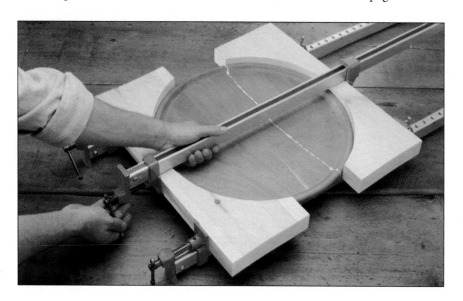

Along with a pair of shop-made clamping blocks, three bar clamps are being used to glue up a split circular tabletop. Cut on the band saw to match the curve of the top, the blocks ensure that uniform clamping pressure is applied along the length of the split.

FLATTENING A CUPPED TOP: USING BATTENS

Installing a batten

To flatten a badly warped tabletop, installing wedges *(page 47)* is the best solution. For a slightly cupped top, try fastening wood battens to its underside. For a batten, select a board that is also slightly cupped. (Once the batten is screwed down flat against the top the tension in the wood will help hold the top flat.) To prepare the batten, counterbore screw holes through it: one at the middle, one near each end, and one every 3 to 4 inches in between. Use a file to elongate the top half of each hole except for the middle one; this will enable the top to move with changes in humidity. Then clamp the top face-down to a work surface and position the batten over the cupped section so that it cups in the opposite direction. Drill pilot holes into the top and screw the batten in place *(right)*, making sure the screws do not penetrate the top surface.

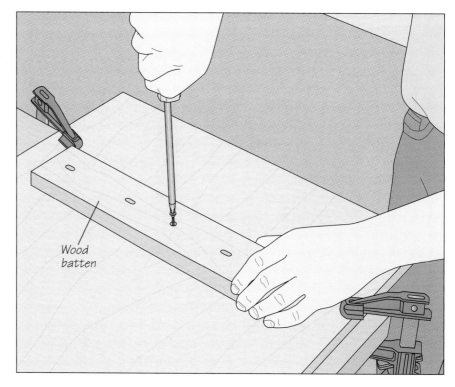

Wood batten

FLATTENING A CUPPED TOP: USING WEDGES

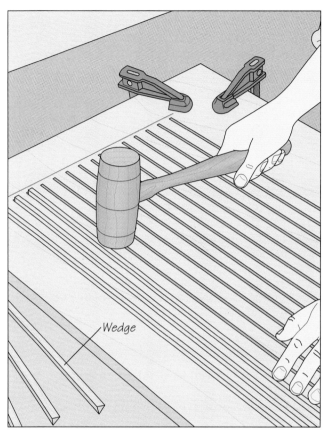

Edge guide

Wedge

1 Preparing the tabletop

For a badly warped top, you need to relieve tension from the underside to allow the top to be forced flat. Clamp the top face-down to a work surface and mark a line across the surface about 1 inch from each end. Adjust a circular saw to make a cut two-thirds through the top and make a series of kerfs along the length of the workpiece, starting and finishing about 2 inches from each edge. Clamp an edge guide to the top to guide each cut *(above)*. Space the kerfs at 1-inch intervals. Square the ends of the kerfs with a chisel.

2 Gluing in wedges

Once all the kerfs have been cut, use as many clamps as necessary to flatten the top down on the work surface. Then use wedges to keep the top flat. Cut one for each kerf, making the length equal to that of the kerf and the thickness slightly wider than the kerf width. The wedges should be sized so they protrude slightly above the surface of the table when they are hammered in place. Spread glue on the wedges and in the kerfs, and tap them in position with a wooden mallet *(above)*. Once the glue has cured, trim the wedges flush with the underside of the top and sand the surface smooth.

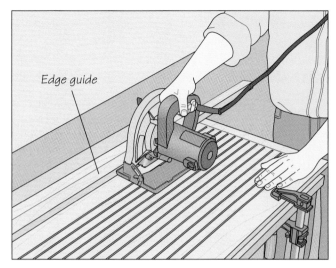

SHOP TIP

Kerfing a tabletop with a router
Instead of cutting kerfs in the underside of a cupped tabletop with a circular saw, you can use a router fitted with a ⅛-inch up-cut spiral bit. Although you still need an edge guide to feed the tool in a straight line, the router offers two advantages for this operation. First, you can cut the kerfs closer to the ends of the top and, second, you do not need to square the ends of the kerfs by hand. For deep cuts, make the kerfs with a series of successively deeper passes.

REPAIRING A SPLIT TOP

Using veneer shims

To repair minor surface cracks and blemishes in tabletops, such as gouges, dents, and scratches, use a wood-patching compound *(page 102)*. For splits right through the thickness of the top, make the repair with veneer shims. Select a filler wood that matches the original color as closely as possible; for wide cracks, try to match the top's grain pattern as well. Taper and sand the shim to fit in the split tightly, spread glue on the piece, and tap it into the opening with a wooden mallet *(right)*. In placing the shim, take care not to further expand the split; fill, but do not force, the defect. Trim the shim flush with the surface, then sand the area smooth.

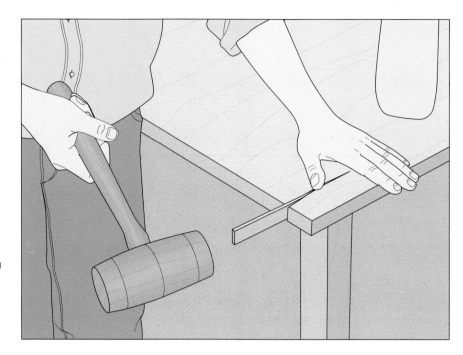

REPLACING AN INLAID LEATHER DESKTOP

 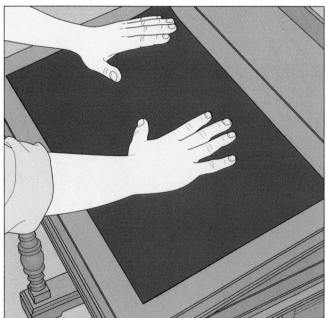

1 Gluing down the new inlay

Remove the damaged leather inlay from the desktop and repair any defects in the suface. Then cut a new piece of leather ½ inch longer and wider than the recess. Spread hide glue on the desk surface *(above, left)* and the under-side of the inlay, and center the leather in the recess, pressing it down as flat as possible to smooth out any wrinkles *(above, right)*. (Some woodworkers use thick wallpaper paste to attach the inlay.)

2 Rolling and trimming the leather

As soon as the inlay is in position, use a hand roller to flatten it out, eliminating any wrinkles or air bubbles. Starting in the center of the inlay, roll out to the edges and ends, applying moderate pressure *(right)*; avoid pressing too hard or stretching the leather. To trim the inlay, run a fingernail along the edges of the recess, scoring the leather, then cut along the score line with a surgeon's scalpel or a razor-sharp craft knife. Angle the blade toward the center of the inlay and cut with a downward stroke so that only the finished surface of the leather shows around the edges. Once the trimming is done, press the edges firmly down with your thumb, then hand-roll the surface again. Treat the leather with glycerine saddle soap or a solution of one part anhydrous lanolin and three parts neatsfoot oil, and reapply once a year.

REPAIRING A DAMAGED TRIPOD TABLE LEG

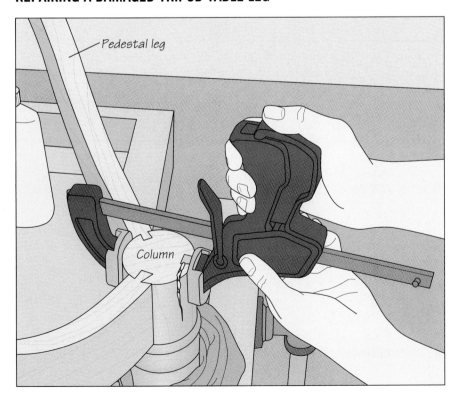

Pedestal leg

Column

1 Repairing the column

The legs of a tripod table are typically joined to the column with sliding dovetails, as shown at left. When a leg breaks off from the column, it usually opens a crack in it. To reattach the leg, start by fixing the column. Secure the table upside down in a bench vise, wrapping a cloth around the column to protect it from the vise jaws. Spread glue on both sides of the split and use a clamp to hold the pieces together *(left)*.

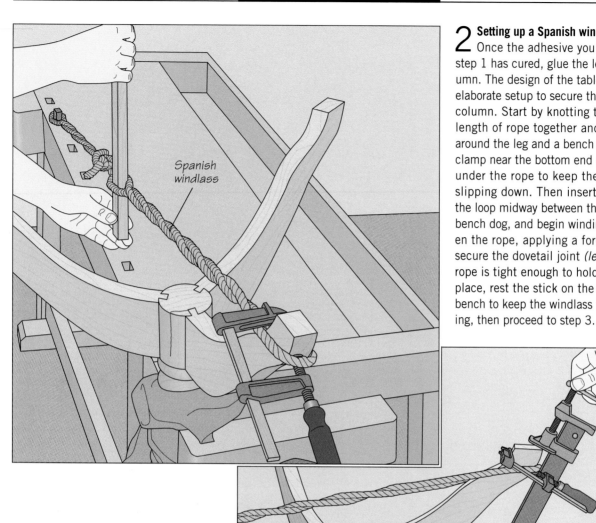

Spanish windlass

2 Setting up a Spanish windlass

Once the adhesive you applied in step 1 has cured, glue the leg to the column. The design of the table calls for an elaborate setup to secure the leg to the column. Start by knotting the ends of a length of rope together and looping it around the leg and a bench dog. Install a clamp near the bottom end of the leg just under the rope to keep the loop from slipping down. Then insert a stick into the loop midway between the leg and the bench dog, and begin winding it to tighten the rope, applying a force that will secure the dovetail joint *(left)*. Once the rope is tight enough to hold the leg in place, rest the stick on the edge of the bench to keep the windlass from unwinding, then proceed to step 3.

3 Balancing the clamping pressure

Relying solely on the Spanish windlass to secure the pedestal leg will apply excess clamping pressure on the heel of the joint—or bottom end of the column. To equalize the pressure, use a bar clamp, placing one jaw on the tip of the leg and the other jaw on the top of the column. Alternate tightening the bar clamp *(right)* and the windlass so the joint closes squarely and glue squeezes out of it.

REPAIRING A DAMAGED PEDESTAL TABLE LEG: DOWEL JOINT

1 Repairing a split leg

On a pedestal table, the legs are often connected to the column with dowels; a break in a joint often results in a split leg. Mend the leg before reattaching it to the column. Spread glue on the contacting surfaces, fit them together and secure the leg in a bench vise. To apply clamping pressure along the entire length of the glue bond and prevent the leg from slipping out of the vise, you may need to install a second clamp. In the setup shown at right, an angled block is clamped to the outside of the vise. This allows the second clamp to be installed squarely, with one jaw on the curved edge of the leg and the other jaw on the clamping block.

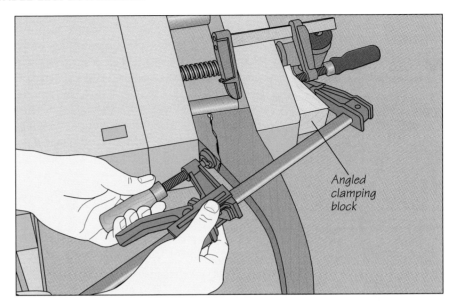

Angled clamping block

Stop collar

2 Preparing the column and legs

On the table shown, all four legs have been detached and must be reinstalled. Start by removing the original dowels or cutting them flush with the surfaces of the column and legs. In the latter case, you need to drill new dowel holes. Fit a drill with a bit the same diameter as the dowels you will use and install a stop collar on the bit to mark the drilling depth—slightly more than one-half the dowel length. For the column, clamp the assembly upside down on a work surface and drill a hole at each dowel location (above). Repeat for each leg.

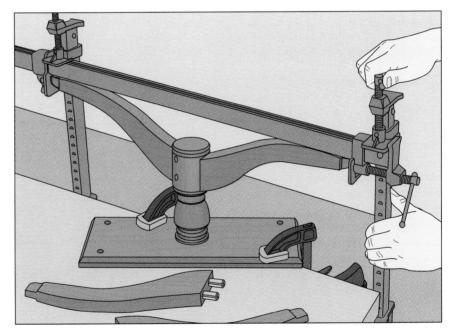

3 Installing the legs

On a pedestal table, glue the legs to the column in pairs. Dab some glue in the dowel holes in the column and two of the legs, insert the dowels in the leg holes and fit the legs in place. Clamp the legs in two steps, starting by installing a long bar clamp across the tips of opposing legs. This clamp will force the legs up and away from the column. To offset this effect, add another clamp at each end of the first clamp, securing it to the work surface. Tighten the vertical clamps so the horizontal clamp is level and the dowel joints are snug (above). Once the glue has cured, repeat the process to attach the remaining legs, repositioning the setup on the work surface, if necessary, to clear the clamps.

REPAIRING CHAIRS

Chairs are subjected to almost constant abuse. Even when they are simply sat upon, the passage of time is often enough to loosen joints, break legs, and split backs or armrests. But when chairs are tilted back on their rear legs or used as makeshift stepladders, the added stress can cause all sorts of damage.

The remaining pages of this chapter show you how to repair many of the problems that typically afflict chairs, such as broken or split legs *(below)*, loose rungs *(page 55)*, and cracked seats *(page 58)*. Refer to the Repairing Joints chapter *(page 24)* for instructions on fixing the joints commonly seen on chairs, including mortise-and-tenons.

Not all chair seats are made from solid wood. Although cane, rush, and upholstered seats are sturdy and durable, they will eventually need to be redone. Beginning on page 61 are step-by-step procedures for redoing these types of chair seats.

Some furniture repairs, particularly when curved parts are involved, require ingenious clamping setups. To secure the armrest—which was split in half at the middle—to the frame chair shown at left, four clamps are needed. The bar clamp at the front is installed vertically to secure the arm to the front leg; the next clamp holds a curved clamping block for the bar clamp, and the third clamp secures another clamping block for the last clamp, which presses the arm against the rear leg.

FIXING A BROKEN TURNED LEG

1 Gluing and clamping the leg
Cut out any splinters from the broken section and secure the leg in a bench vise so the split is fully exposed. Spread glue on both sides of the break then, squeezing the split closed, clamp it with a length of surgical tubing, available at woodworking supply centers. Starting about 1 inch before the break, begin wrapping the tubing tightly around the leg; overlap the first loop to hold the tubing in place. Continue, spacing the wraps about ½ inch apart *(right)*, until you are about 1 inch beyond the break. Cut the tubing and tuck the end under the last loop to secure it. Let the glue cure.

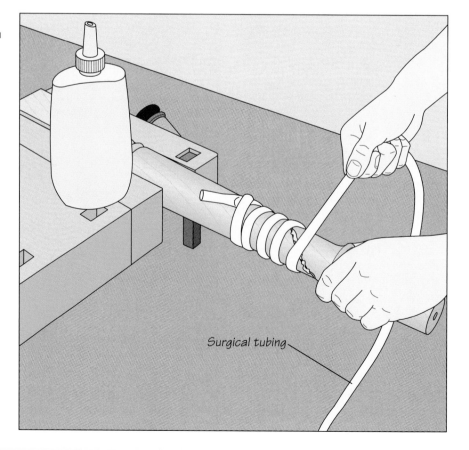

Surgical tubing

2 Preparing the leg for a dowel

If the leg is fractured straight across you will need to reinforce the repaired leg with a dowel glued up through its center. (A fracture at an oblique angle will provide enough glue surface to form a bond that will not require any reinforcement.) Leaving the surgical tubing on the leg, fit a ratcheting hand brace with a ⁷⁄₁₆- or ½-inch electrician's bit. These long bits will enable you to bore a hole deep enough to pass through the repaired leg section. Mark the center of the leg's end and position the tip of the bit on your mark. Pressing the head of the brace with your hip, grip the handle with one hand and the chuck with the other, and crank the handle to bore the hole *(right)*. Drill as deeply as the bit will reach—without penetrating the opposite end—keeping the brace level throughout.

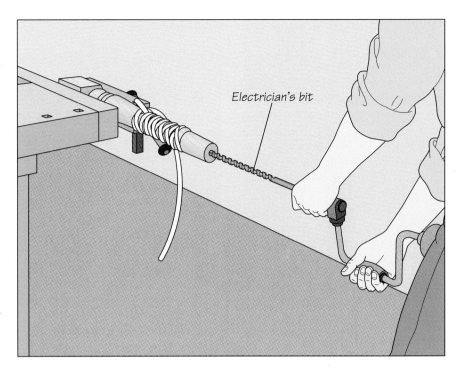

Electrician's bit

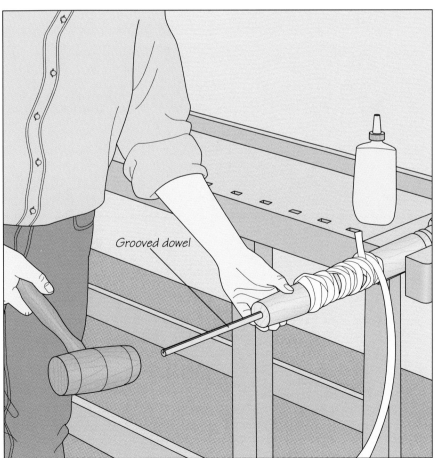

Grooved dowel

3 Inserting the dowel

To allow excess glue to escape from the hole in the leg, groove the dowel you will using. Bore a hole in a scrap piece, drive a screw into an edge so that the tip extends into the hole, and pass the dowel through the hole. You can also carve a groove by clamping the dowel in a vise and using a chisel. Then spread glue on the dowel and use a wooden mallet to tap it in place *(left)*. Trim the dowel flush with the end of the leg and sand the surface smooth.

REPAIRING A SPLIT CABRIOLE LEG

1 Reattaching the toe

The toe has split from the foot and ankle of the cabriole leg illustrated on this page—a common injury on older chairs. The leg shown is also detached from the chair frame; to reattach it, refer to the Repairing Joints chapter *(page 24)*. Carefully remove any crossed fibers from both sides of the break, then secure the leg bottom-end-up in a bench vise. Dry-fit the toe against the leg, spread glue on the contacting surfaces, and use a handscrew to clamp the toe in place *(right)*.

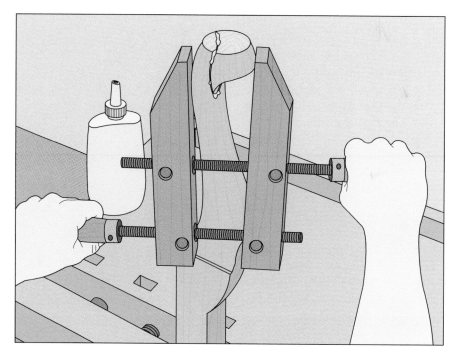

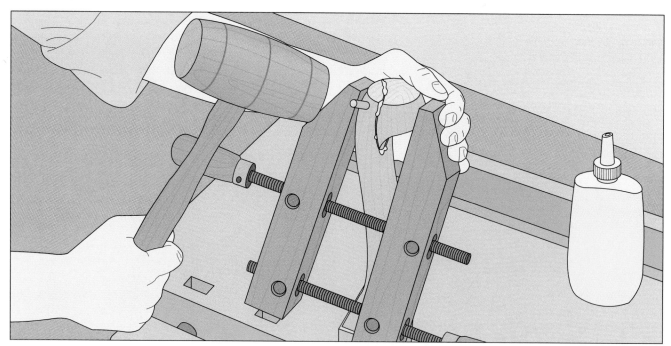

2 Reinforcing the repair

To strengthen the bond between toe and leg, drive a dowel through the joint. Leaving the leg in the vise and the handscrew on the leg, use an electric drill to bore a dowel hole into the leg. Start the hole at the back of the leg so the end of the dowel will be inconspicuous; stop drilling before the bit penetrates the front of the toe. To avoid weakening the repair, make sure the dowel is not too large. Cut the dowel slightly longer than the hole depth, spread glue on it, and tap it into the hole with a wooden mallet *(above)*. Trim the dowel flush with the surface and sand the repair smooth.

TIGHTENING A LOOSE STRETCHER

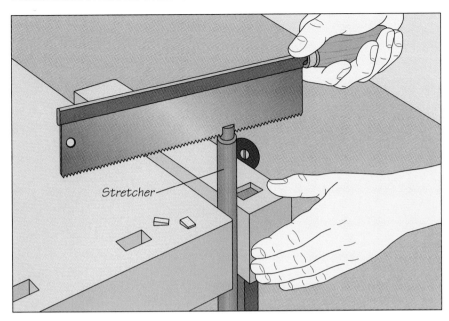

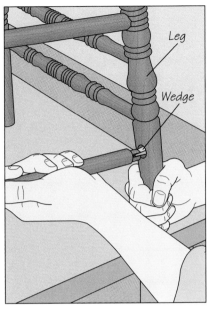

1 Kerfing the stretcher tenon

Chair stretchers are typically joined to the legs with round mortise-and-tenons. To reattach a loose stretcher, kerf its tenons and insert hidden wedges; a wedge will expand a tenon and tighten its fit. Secure the stretcher end-up in a bench vise and use a backsaw to cut the kerf from the tip to the shoulder of each tenon. Keep the blade perpendicular to the workpiece and make the cut across the middle of the tenon *(above)*.

2 Reattaching the stretcher

Cut each wedge to reach from the bottom of its mortise in the leg to the tenon shoulder. If the wedge is too long, it will be impossible to set the stretcher in place, or—worse—split the stretcher; if the wedge is too short, it will not expand the tenon enough. Once the wedges are ready, insert them into their tenons and spread glue on the stretcher tenons and in the leg mortises. Spread the legs apart slightly, then fit the tenons into the mortises one at a time *(above)*, rotating the stretcher so the wedge is perpendicular to the grain of the leg. Close the joints snugly with a dead-blow hammer.

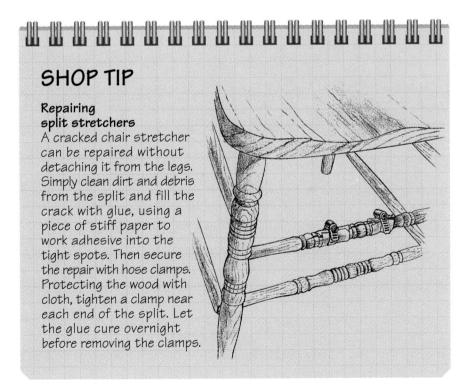

SHOP TIP

Repairing split stretchers

A cracked chair stretcher can be repaired without detaching it from the legs. Simply clean dirt and debris from the split and fill the crack with glue, using a piece of stiff paper to work adhesive into the tight spots. Then secure the repair with hose clamps. Protecting the wood with cloth, tighten a clamp near each end of the split. Let the glue cure overnight before removing the clamps.

REPAIRING A SPLIT IN BENT WOOD

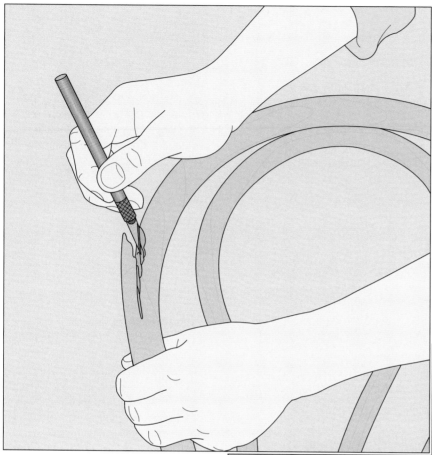

1 Preparing the split
To help the sides of the crack bond together properly, use a sharp craft knife to clean dirt out of the break and cut away any loose splinters *(left)*. Work carefully to avoid marring any surface that will be visible after the repair is completed.

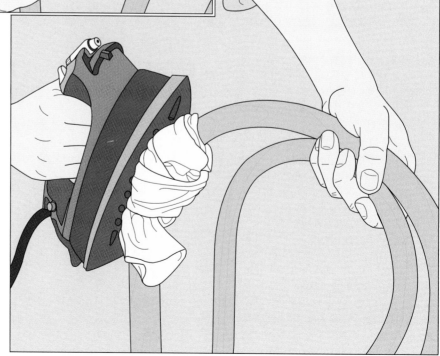

2 Softening the wood
The broken parts cannot be bent back into their original position permanently unless the wood on each side of the break is first steamed and softened. To localize the steaming to the wood surrounding the split, soak a cloth in hot water, and wrap it around the damaged area. Then adjust a household iron to its highest setting and pass the iron back and forth on the cloth *(right)*. Continue until the wood is pliable enough to be pressed back into shape; this should take about 15 minutes. Do not let the cloth dry out; sprinkle water on it, as necessary. Once the wood is sufficiently bendable, remove the cloth and proceed quickly to step 3.

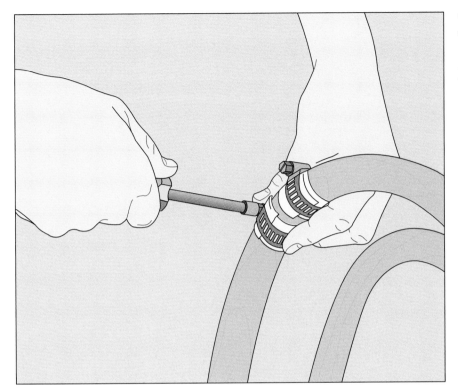

3 Gluing the split

Protecting the wood with strips of cloth, use as many hose clamps as necessary to bend the softened wood and close the break. Tighten the clamps with a screwdriver or nutdriver *(left)*. Leave the clamps in place for 24 hours, allowing the wood to dry and maintain its bent shape. When you remove the clamps, however, the break should spring open enough for you to spread glue on both sides of the split. Use a piece of stiff paper to work adhesive into the tight spots, then reinstall the hose clamps.

4 Reinforcing the repair

If the break in the wood penetrated more than one-quarter of the way through its thickness, reinforce your repair with dowels. Use an electric drill to bore holes for ⅛-inch dowels spaced every 2 inches along the repair. Stop drilling before the bit penetrates the opposite side of the stock. Cut each dowel slightly longer than the hole depth, spread glue on it and tap it into the hole with a wooden mallet *(right)*. Use a fine-toothed saw, such as a dovetail saw, to trim the dowels flush with the surface, then sand the area smooth.

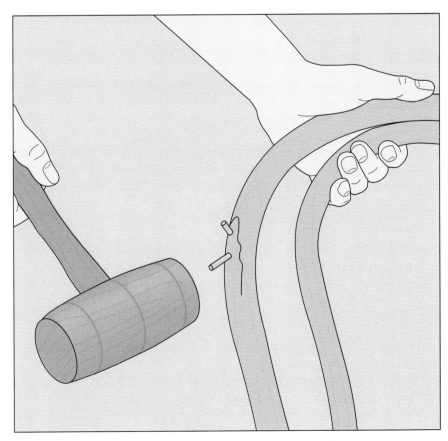

REPAIRING A CRACKED SEAT

1 Making the butterfly keys
To reinforce a split chair seat that has been glued back together, use butterfly keys. Start by securing the chair seat upside down on a work surface, spreading glue on both sides of the split and using bar clamps to secure the joint, as shown below. If the two sides of the break do not lie perfectly level with each other, use another clamp to hold them in alignment. Protect the stock from the clamp jaws with wood pads. To make the butterfly keys, plane a hardwood strip to about one-quarter the thickness of the seat and rip it to a width of about 1 inch. Outline two keys on the strip, angling the "wings" at 10°. Once the keys are outlined, cut them from the strip on your band saw *(right)* and bevel their edges slightly with a chisel.

2 Outlining the keys on the seat
Center one of the butterfly keys on the glue line of the repair and use a pencil to outline its shape on the underside of the seat. Repeat for the other key *(below)*. Position the keys about 6 inches in from the ends of the seat and 6 to 8 inches apart. (Note that the armrest has been removed from the chair shown.)

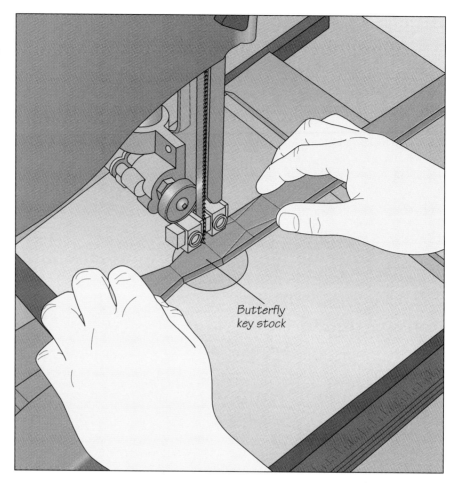

Butterfly key stock

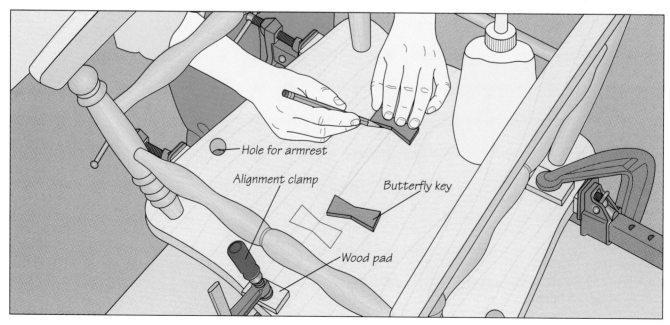

Hole for armrest

Alignment clamp

Butterfly key

Wood pad

3 Making the recesses

Remove most of the waste wood from the recesses for the butterfly keys using a router, then finish the job with a chisel. Install a ¼-inch straight bit in the router and set the cutting depth to slightly less than the thickness of the keys. This is one of the rare cases when a router is used to make a freehand cut; care and patience are required. Guide the tool against the direction of bit rotation to clear out the waste in the middle of the recesses *(right)*, but do not attempt to cut right up to the outlines. Use a chisel to square the corners and pare to the lines.

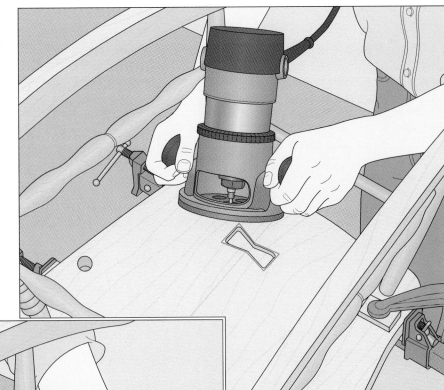

4 Installing the butterfly keys

Test-fit the keys in their recesses and bevel the undersides if necessary to improve the fit. Then spread glue in the recesses and insert the keys, tapping them in place with a wooden mallet *(left)*. Once the glue has cured, use sandpaper or a dogleg chisel to trim the keys flush with the seat surface. Note that you can also use this method to strengthen a repair to a split tabletop.

GLUING UP CHAIRS

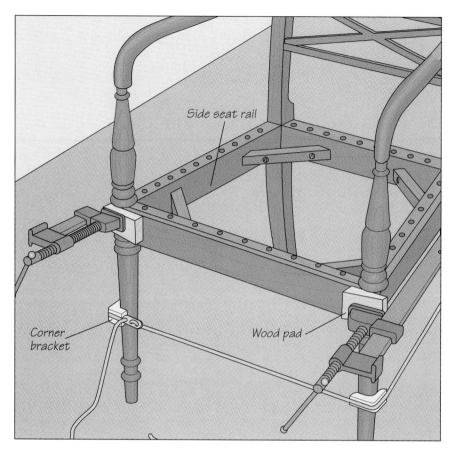

Side seat rail

Corner
bracket

Wood pad

Clamping a frame chair
The legs are typically joined to the seat rails of frame chairs with mortise-and-tenons. To repair a chair in which a leg has separated from the rails, spread adhesive on the contacting surfaces of the pieces and use the clamping setup shown at left to glue up the legs and rails. Install a pair of bar clamps on the legs, protecting the stock with wood pads as wide as the rails and aligning the clamp bars with the side rails. To prevent the legs from being forced out of alignment, install a web clamp with corner brackets around the legs about halfway up the legs. The brackets help to distribute the clamping pressure evenly.

Clamping a stick chair
The legs of stick chairs are usually attached to the rails and stretchers with round mortise-and-tenon joints. To glue up a stick chair, spread glue on all the mating surfaces of the legs, rails, and stretchers, then wrap a web clamp around the legs about two-thirds of the way up the legs, as shown at right. Make sure the clamp is tightened snugly.

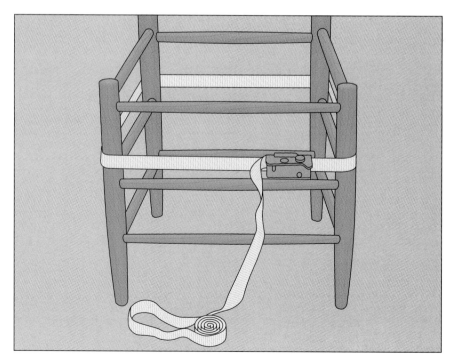

REPAIRING CANE SEATS

The delicate appearance of a woven cane seat belies its durability, but eventually the cane becomes worn and breaks, and the seat must be replaced. Recaning is time-consuming—it can take up to 12 hours to weave a seat for a typical chair—but the result can be both elegant and faithful to the original. Start the process by making any needed repairs to the seat frame that anchors the cane.

Cane is usually sold in bundles called hanks, made of 10- to 20-foot lengths totaling 1000 feet. This is usually enough for about four chairs with 12-inch-square caned panels. The chart on page 62 shows the various widths of cane available and the diameter of the holes in the frame that accept the various strand widths. Measure the diameter of the holes in the frame of the chair you are recaning to determine the strand width you need. The only other supplies required are special wooden pegs to hold the strands of cane in the holes as you weave them; you can make them from dowels, or even use golf tees.

To keep the strands flexible, place them in a bucket of warm water. Glycerine can be added to make the cane easier to thread. Should a length dry and become brittle as you weave it, you can sponge a bit of water on it. Always keep the cane's glossy side up. Do not allow the cane to twist, especially under the seat frame or in the holes. Also, the cane can only be woven in one direction; otherwise, it will catch and break. Run a fingernail along the glossy side and you will notice a bump every foot or so. Each bump is a leaf node. Your nail will catch on the nodes in one direction, but not in the other. Weave the cane in the direction that allows you to pull the leaf nodes through the holes without catching. When a length of cane comes to an end, peg it in a hole, trim it to leave an excess of about 5 inches, and start a new length up through the adjacent hole.

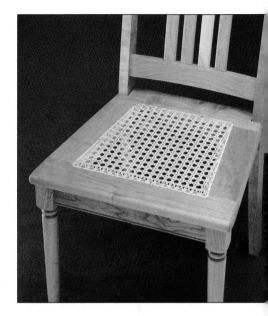

Recaning a chair seat is a time-consuming process but not difficult to master. The result is a seat that can last for decades. The strands of rattan can be woven in a variety of patterns, as shown in the illustration below.

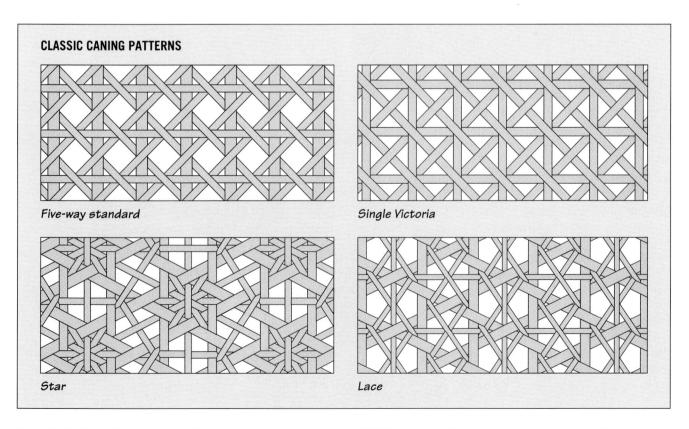

CLASSIC CANING PATTERNS

Five-way standard

Single Victoria

Star

Lace

CANE SIZE	ACTUAL WIDTHS	METRIC WIDTH	HOLE DIAMETER	HOLES CENTER TO CENTER
Super Fine		2 mm	1/8"	3/8"
Fine Fine		2.25 mm	3/16"	1/2"
Fine		2.5 mm	3/16"	5/8"
Narrow Medium		2.75 mm	1/4"	3/4"
Medium		3 mm	1/4"	3/4"
Common		3.5 mm	5/16"	7/8"

WEAVING THE CANE

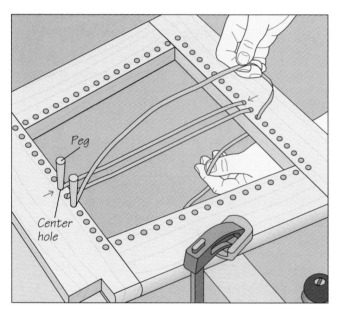

1 Weaving the first vertical rows

Clamp the caning frame to a workbench so that the holes are unobstructed. Then take a length of cane from your bucket and feed it from above into the center hole in the back frame piece. Leave about 5 inches hanging below the frame and insert a peg into the hole to secure the strand. Now bring the strand across the frame and through the top of the center hole in the front piece; pull it fairly taut and peg it. (You should be able to deflect the center of the strand an inch or so.) Pass the strand up through the adjacent hole on the front piece and bring it across to the back piece, feeding it down from the top into the hole next to where you started. Continue in this fashion *(left)*, moving one hole sideways and up and then across the frame, always transferring the peg from the last hole. Leave the first peg in place as well as any peg securing the end or start of a strand.

2 Keeping the rows parallel

If your caning frame is trapezoidal rather than square, as in the example shown here, you will have to peg some strands in a hole in the side piece, rather than the front or back, as you reach the side of the frame. This will keep the last row parallel to the preceding ones. When you get to the side piece, choose the appropriate hole and and feed the cane into it as described in step 1 *(right)*. Once this is done, return to the hole adjacent to where you started and weave the cane toward the opposite side. Remember to peg the cane at the beginning and end of each strand, leaving about 5 inches hanging below the frame.

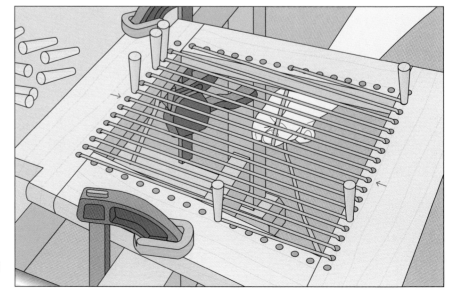

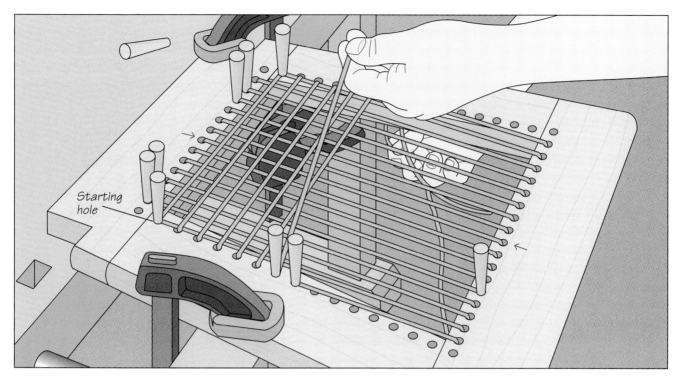

3 Installing the first horizontal rows

Once the first set of vertical rows has been installed, move on to the first horizontal row. Start with the first hole in one side piece at the back of the frame. Remove the peg from the hole if there is one, then feed the cane up through the hole and insert a peg to secure the strand. Pull the strand over the frame and the vertical rows already in place, and secure the cane in the first hole in the opposite side piece, using a peg. Continue to weave horizontal rows as you did the vertical rows *(above)*, working from the back toward the front of the frame.

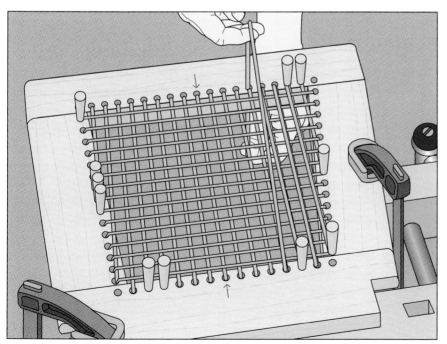

4 Adding the second vertical rows

Weave the second vertical row as you did the first, passing the cane over all the strands in place. However, instead of starting at the middle of the back rail, begin with the last hole you pegged in the first vertical row in the left-hand side of the seat frame. Then, weave the cane from this point *(left)* toward the opposite side, aligning the strands slightly to the right of the first set of vertical strands.

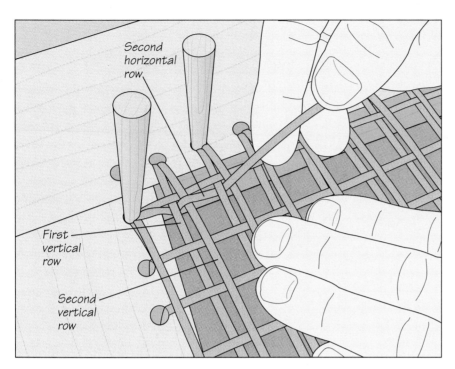

Second horizontal row

First vertical row

Second vertical row

5 **Weaving the second horizontal rows**
Now the weaving begins with the second horizontal row. Start with the same hole in which you started the first horizontal row and peg the strand in place. Then, weave the cane under the first vertical row and over the second one, positioning the cane beside the first horizontal row *(left)*. Continue weaving in this way until you reach the seat front, and peg the last strand in place.

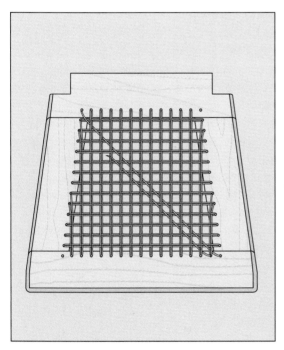

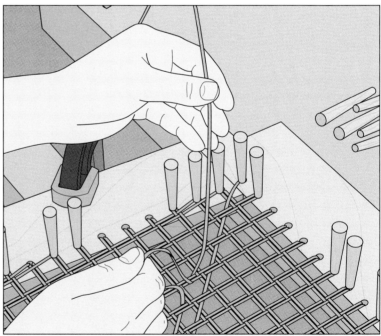

6 **Weaving the first diagonal rows**
Peg a length of cane in one of the corner holes at the back of the frame. Pass the cane over the horizontal strands and under the vertical strands to the immediate right *(above, left)*. Continue until you reach the opposite corner hole. Then pass the strand up through the hole in the front frame piece next to the corner hole and work your way toward the back of the seat, weaving the cane under the vertical rows and over the horizontal ones *(above, right)*. Continue weaving diagonal rows this way until you reach the other corner hole in the front of the seat, making sure that all the rows are parallel. Now, return to the hole in the back of the chair frame next to where you started the diagonal rows and repeat the process, working in the opposite direction.

7 Weaving the second diagonal rows

Start the second diagonal weave in the left-hand corner hole in the front of the chair frame. This time, feed the cane over the vertical rows and under the horizontal ones *(right)*. Complete the rows as in step 6.

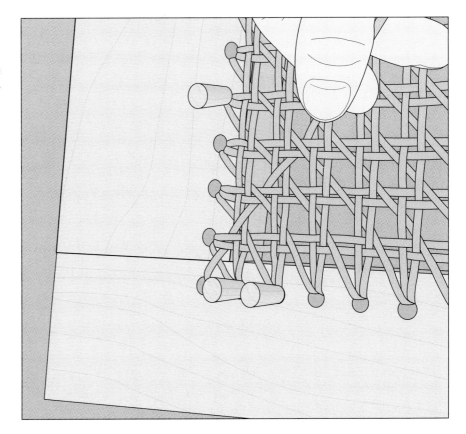

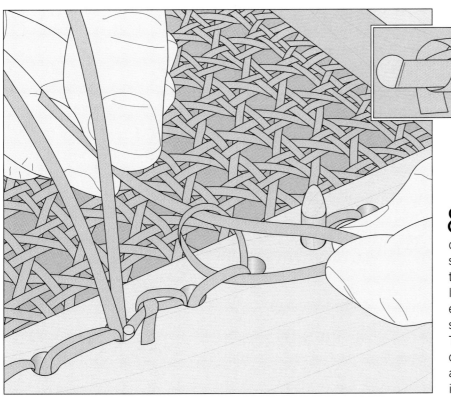

8 Tying off the loose ends of cane

Once the second diagonal row is done, it is time to secure the loose strands hanging under the frame. Turn the seat frame over and use the double-loop knot shown in the inset to secure each strand. To tie this knot, slip a loose strand under an adjacent strap of cane. Then feed it through the loop you just created *(left)*, pass it under the strap again and cinch it tight. Trim the remaining portion, leaving a ½-inch-long tip.

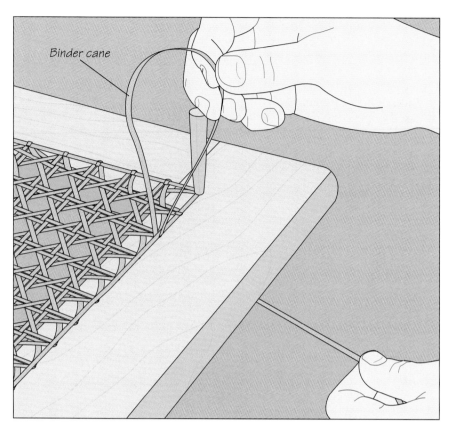

Binder cane

9 Appplying the binder cane

Once the weaving is done and all the ends have been tied-off, apply a strip of binder cane around the perimeter of the seat to give it a neat and finished appearance. Binder cane is usually one or two sizes larger than the cane used for the weave. Pass the end of the binder cane down through the left-back corner hole and peg it in place. Lay the binder cane across the row of holes in the back frame piece, then use a length of weaving cane smaller than the one you used for the seat to anchor the binder cane. Tie loops over the binder cane by passing the weaving strand up through the first hole adjacent to the corner, over the binder cane, and back down through the same hole *(left)*. Move on to the next hole in the back of the seat frame and repeat, continuing until you reach the corner hole at the end of the piece. Trim off the excess length of binder cane and use new lengths along the remaining frame pieces.

10 Pegging the corners

Once all the binder cane is installed, tie off the ends of the weaving cane you used to anchor it. At each corner, pull the binder cane taut and temporarily tap a peg into the corner hole. Mark the peg at the point where it meets the top of the frame piece, remove the peg and trim it at the mark. Spread a little glue on the sides of the peg and tap it in place with a hammer *(right)*. Then trim the peg flush with the surface using a chisel.

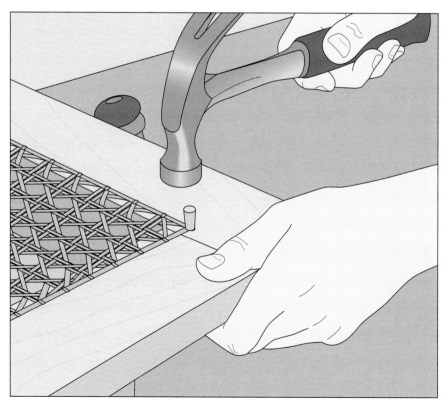

REPAIRING A RUSH SEAT

Rush for chair seats was traditionally made of twisted cattail leaves. Today, it is more common to weave a seat with a tough-grade, fibrous paper twisted into long strands, known as "fiber rush." Although an antique chair may have used natural rush, weaving a seat with this material takes time to learn as well as an understanding of how to harvest and prepare the leaves. If you are rushing a seat for the first time, it is best to master the fiber-paper rush technique shown below and on the following pages before tackling natural rush.

Fiber rush is sold by the pound and comes in three sizes: ³⁄₃₂ inch for fine work, ⁵⁄₃₂ inch for most chairs, and ⁶⁄₃₂ inch for larger pieces and patio furniture. Craft supply dealers are usually good sources of advice for the appropriate size and the amount of rush needed for a partic-

ular project. Try using rush that matches the original as closely as possible. If there is no material left on the seat, you can narrow down your choice by measuring how much the legs extend above the rails. If the measurement is ¼ inch or less, use fine rush; if it is 1 inch or more, select a thicker rush. Before applying rush to a seat frame, make sure all repairs to the frame have been done and the glue has cured completely. The rush will exert moderate tension on the joints when it is installed.

Rushing a chair seat is simpler than caning since it involves repeating a single technique all around the seat frame. Rush works best on chairs with square seats. Seats that are not square can still be rushed, as long as you lay down a few preliminary weaves across the side and front rails to create parallel sides, as shown below.

Before starting, spray the individual lengths of rush with water to keep them pliable. Always pull the rush tightly around the rails and keep adjacent rows as close together as possible.

A simple rush seat can give a charming old chair, like the one shown above, a new lease on life.

RUSHING A CHAIR SEAT

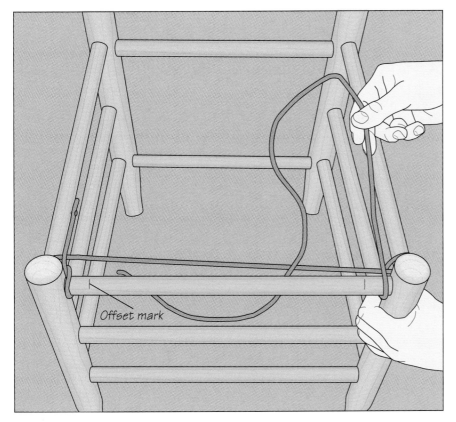

Offset mark

1 Bridging the front rail
If the seat rails do not form a square, you will need to use rush to create a square frame. Measure the difference in length between the longer and shorter rails—in this case, the front and back rails—and divide your measurement in half. Measure your result along the front rail from each of the front legs and make a mark on the rail. Tack a length of dampened rushing that is about twice the length of the front rail to the inside of a side rail about 2 inches from the front leg. Now loop the rush around the front rail from underneath, then around the side rail from underneath. Bring the rush across the front rail and loop it around the other side rail and the front rail *(left)*. Holding the rush taut, tack it to the side rail opposite the first tack.

2 Squaring the seat frame

Fasten a length of rush alongside the first one, using the technique described in step 1. Loop it around the front and side rails and fasten it to the opposite rail. Continue adding lengths of rush *(right)* until you reach the offset marks you made on the front rail. Be sure to keep the rush as tight and straight as possible.

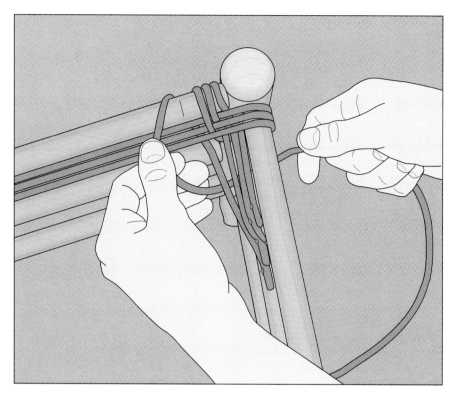

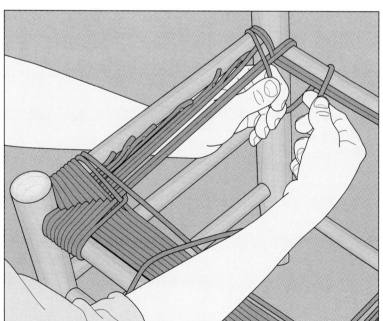

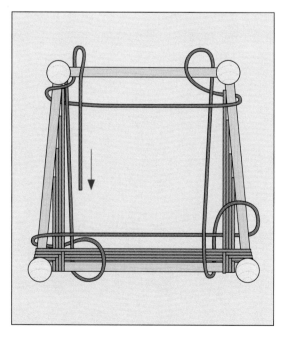

3 Weaving a complete circuit

Once you have squared the seat frame, you can begin rushing the seat all around the frame. Working with an approximately 20-foot length of rush, tack it to the side rail near the rear legs and loop it around all the rails *(above, left)*. Each complete circuit is known as a bout. Keep working around the chair using the same pattern *(above, right)*. When you get to the end of a length of rush, clamp it temporarily to the seat frame to keep it taut and attach it to a new piece using a figure-eight knot. Locate the knots on the underside of the seat so they will not be visible.

4 Checking the weave for square
Once every third or fourth circuit, check whether the sides of the seat are perpendicular to each other. Holding the length of rush in a coil with one hand, butt a try square in one corner of the seat *(right)*. The handle and blade of the square should rest flush against the rushing. If not, use a flat-tip screwdriver to straighten the side that is out-of-square, pushing the last circuit you installed against adjacent ones. Repeat at the remaining corners of the seat.

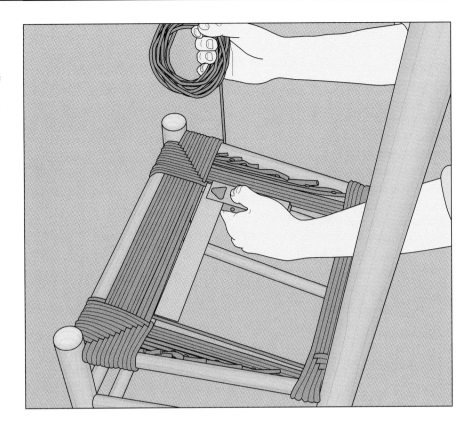

5 Stuffing the seat
Once the rushing is about two-thirds done, it is time to stuff the seat. The stuffing provides extra padding. To prevent the rush from slackening, use a spring clamp to secure the loose length you are installing to a seat rail. Use cardboard for the padding, cutting one triangular piece for each each side of the seat so that the triangle's long side is slightly shorter than the seat rail. Slip the padding under the rushing *(left)*, then trim the tips if they overlap in the center. Continue the normal circuit as before until the two side rails are covered.

Spring clamp

6 Completing the bridge

On a seat that is deeper than it is wide, as in the chair shown at right, the rushing being installed on the side rails will meet in the middle of the seat before the rush on the front and back rails. Once this occurs, use a technique known as bridging to fill the gap. Loop the rushing on the front and back rails with a figure-eight pattern weave, passing the rush over the back rail, down through the center, under the seat, and up around the front rail. Then bring the rush over the seat from the front rail and back down through the center *(right)*. Pass the rush under the seat, come up around the back rail again, and repeat.

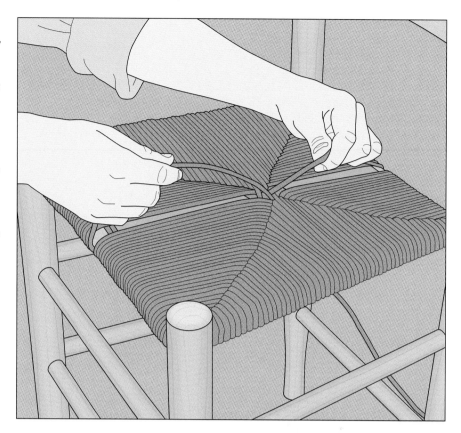

7 Finishing the job

Once you have bridged the gap between the front and back rails, set the chair upside down on a work table, tack the last strand of rush to the underside of the back seat rail *(below)*, and trim it to length.

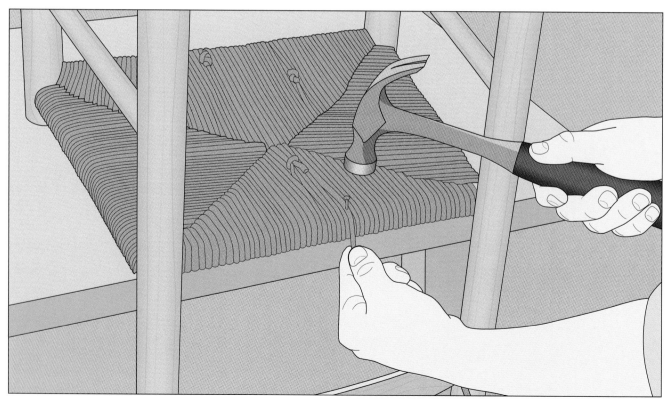

REUPHOLSTERING CHAIR SEATS

Upholstered furniture is so common today that it is hard to imagine that it was once considered a rarity. Yet until the early 1800s, textiles were expensive, and upholstered furniture was normally found only in the homes of the wealthiest people. This changed with the advent of the Industrial Revolution, which helped to make textiles more readily available. Originally, most upholstered furniture was stuffed with horsehair. In the mid 1800s, springs were introduced to underlie the horsehair, and the hair has now been largely superseded by foam rubber.

Upholstery fabric is not nearly as durable as the furniture it covers.

Refurbishing an upholstered chair seat usually involves replacing the wood base, the padding, and the fabric. When choosing the fabric, try to match the original as closely as possible. The seat shown in this section is recessed in the seat rails. This feature allows the rails to frame the pattern of the fabric.

A piece of fabric is fitted over a plywood seat base, which has been padded with upholstery-grade foam. Once the fabric is centered on the seat, it will be folded neatly at the corners and stapled to the underside of the base, as shown on page 73.

MAKING AN UPHOLSTERED CHAIR SEAT

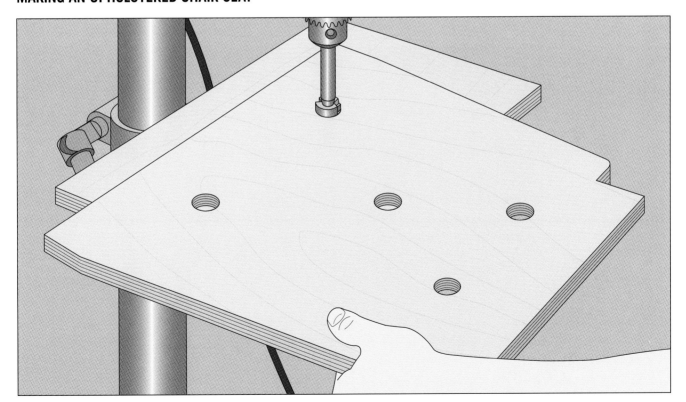

1 Preparing the seat base

Make a plywood or hardboard template of the top surface of the chair's seat rails. If the seat will rest within the rails, make the template ¼ inch smaller than the seat frame to allow for the recess. Trace the outline from the template onto a piece of ½- or ¾-inch plywood and cut it out on your band saw. The plywood will be the seat base. Then insert a large-diameter bit on your drill press and bore several holes through the base *(above)*. The holes will provide ventilation and allow air to escape from the foam padding when the seat is sat on and compressed.

2 Gluing the foam padding to the seat base

Buy a piece of 1½-inch-thick uphol-stery-grade foam padding from a craft supply or hardware store and cut it using a sharp knife to fit over the seat base. A utility knife with a retractable blade will work well for slicing through thick padding. To install the padding, coat the top of the seat base and the underside of the padding with contact cement, let the adhesive dry according to the manufacturer's directions and press the two pieces together *(right)*.

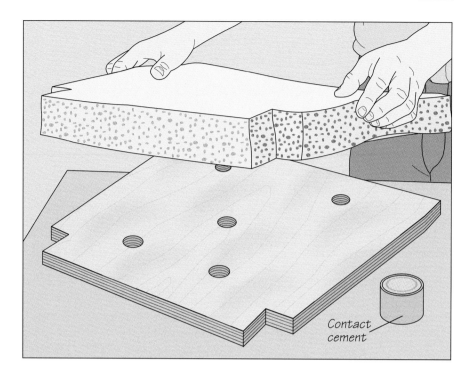

Contact cement

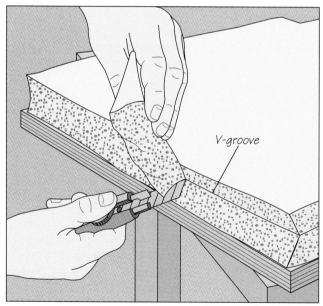

V-groove

3 Trimming the padding

To enable the padding to fold and round over when the fabric covering is applied, cut a V groove into the edges of the foam. Cut into the top of one edge with the utility knife at a 45° angle, penetrating halfway through the pad's thickness. Then run the knife to an adjoining corner, cutting one-half of the groove. Repeat along the bottom of the edge, removing the strip of padding as you go. Cut the groove the same way on the remaining edges of the padding *(above)*.

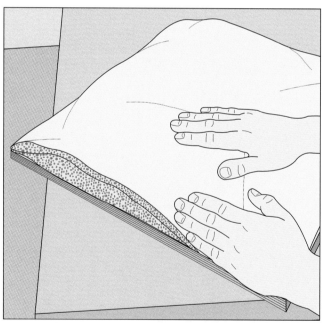

4 Gluing down the edges of the padding

Once all the grooves have been cut into the padding, the edges are ready to be folded down. Apply contact cement to the top and bottom of the grooves, let the adhesive dry, and fold the two parts together *(above)*. Apply hand pressure all around the edges of the padding to ensure uniform and com-plete contact, then use the knife to trim away any padding overhanging the seat base.

5 Installing underlay

Before fastening the fabric covering to the seat, you need to attach a piece of cloth underlay to the base. This will serve as a barrier between the upholstery fabric and the padding, preventing the fabric from adhering to the foam. An old bedsheet is ideal material for the underlay; cut a section several inches larger than the top of the seat. To install it, set the underlay on a work surface and center the seat padded-side down on top. Fold the material over the front of the seat and staple it to the base. Staple the underlay at the back, pulling the material tight and making sure the fabric is neat in the notches for the rear legs. Finally, fasten the underlay over the sides *(right)*. Trim away excess material with scissors.

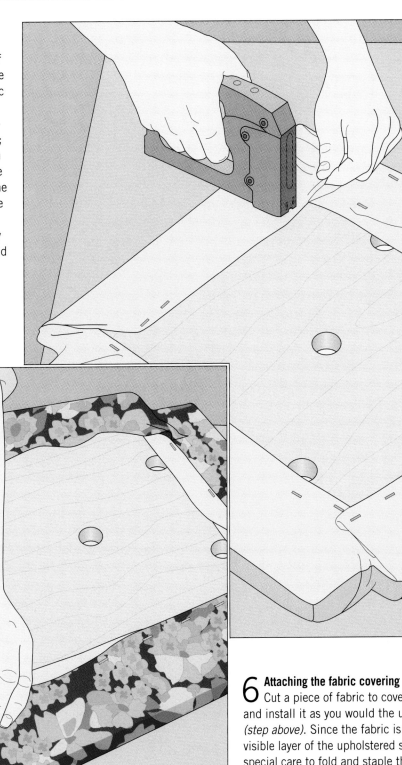

6 Attaching the fabric covering

Cut a piece of fabric to cover the seat and install it as you would the underlay *(step above)*. Since the fabric is the only visible layer of the upholstered seat, take special care to fold and staple the fabric neatly at the corners *(left)*. Once the fabric is attached to the base, fasten the seat to the seat frame, driving the screws from underneath.

RESTORATION TECHNIQUES

Once you have tackled all of the structural repairs required to rehabilitate an antique—such as tightening loose joints, mending a broken leg, or flattening a warped top—you may find that the piece still needs work. A length of molding may be missing from one side, the veneer covering the top may be uneven, or the base of one leg may have broken off. It is remedying faults like these that can make furniture restoration a time-consuming process. However, putting such details right can make the difference between a mere repair job and a restoration. Restoring a piece goes beyond correcting its flaws; it means returning it as closely as possible to its original state.

Missing moldings and badly damaged legs are among the problems that call for making a replacement part. Techniques for replicating several typical furniture parts are shown on pages 76 to 82. Often, the piece itself can serve as your guide in fashioning a new part. There is usually some surviving molding or a matching leg that you can copy. If nothing remains, however, you will have to make

Combining the features of a planer and a shaper, the molding/planer shown above mills a length of molding. The machine works much like a planer, but it can be fitted with custom-ground knives that match the desired profile.

an educated guess. Start by referring to publications, including the Restoration Basics chapter of this book *(page 12)*, that illustrate antique furniture to find a sample that closely matches the piece you are restoring. You can also do some sleuthing at antique stores. You may find a similar piece at a museum.

Pages 83 to 93 describe techniques for correcting flaws such as broken corners and cracked veneer. With many repairs to antiques, it is good practice to finish each task so the repair matches the look of the original; this often means using traditional hand tools because machined surfaces may look too "perfect" for a piece built before the advent of power tools.

Part of the skill of furniture restoration is knowing when to stop and leave a problem alone. Keep in mind that an antique should show signs of its age. Tiny fissures, small surface irregularities, and wormholes are some of the blemishes that add character to a piece. Also, there is always some risk whenever you take a cutting edge to an antique that, without proper care, you will do more harm than good.

A replacement length of molding, shaped with molding cutters on a table saw and with a router, is test-fitted on the pine blanket chest shown at left. Once installed, the molding will be stained and finished to match the original. The chest dates from 1870.

REPLACEMENT PARTS

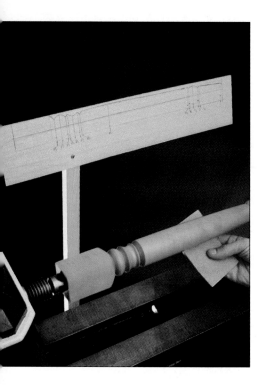

Since one basic rule of furniture restoration is to leave as much of the original intact as possible, making and installing replacement parts should be viewed as a last resort. If the part is missing and it is essential to the function of the piece—a leg for a table or a chair, for example—you have little alternative to reconstructing the absent part. But keep in mind that unless you are faithful to the original, you could lose in authenticity all that you gain in utility. On this and the following page, you will find techniques for reproducing turned and shaped legs.

Often, only the lower part of a leg is damaged and the rest is in good repair.

In such cases, the ideal solution is to replace only the damaged part of the leg and preserve the original portion. Retipping a leg is shown starting on page 78.

In many older pieces, moldings were not installed strictly for decoration, but also to hide the joinery. In practice, they often functioned as bumpers, preventing the edges of the carcase from being damaged. As a result, you will commonly find antique casework with broken and missing strips of molding. There are countless variations in molding styles and it is possible to replicate virtually any one. Refer to page 80 for suggestions on combining table saw molding cutters and router bits to duplicate moldings.

A piece of sandpaper applies the final touches to a leg turned on the lathe. To help reproduce the desired pattern as closely as possible, a scale drawing of the leg should be kept nearby—in this case, attached to a post which is secured to the lathe bed.

REPRODUCING A TURNED LEG

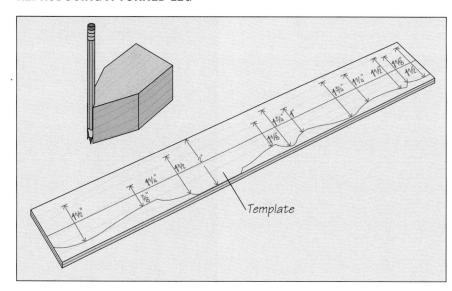

Template

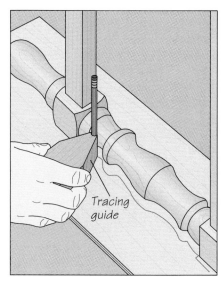

Tracing guide

1 Copying the original design
To reproduce a turned leg, make an accurate template based on a matching leg. One method for transferring the contours of an existing leg onto a template is to use a shop-made tracing guide, like the one shown above, at left. To make the jig, cut a cube from a scrap block, then saw a V in one edge and drill a notch to accommodate a pencil. Glue the pencil in the notch, then set the existing leg on your plywood template,

which should be wider and longer than the leg. To use the guide, hold it flat on the template and guide the pencil along the leg's contours, making sure the point of the V rides against the leg (above, right). Once the leg's profile has been copied, mark a centerline down the middle of the outline and indicate the finished diameter of the leg at each transition point along its length.

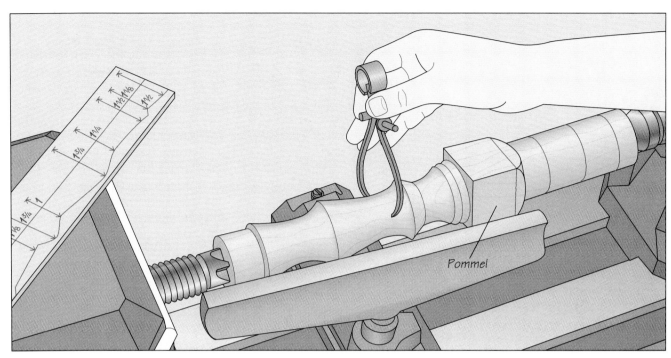

Pommel

2 Turning the replacement leg

Mount a leg blank between centers on your lathe and mark any square sections, or pommels. Use a roughing gouge to turn the remaining portion into a cylinder then, butting the template against the blank, transfer the transition points from the template to the workpiece with a pencil. Use a spindle gouge, a skew chisel, and a parting tool, as necessary, to turn the contours of the leg, checking your progress with calipers *(above)*. Continue until the shape of the leg corresponds to the measurements on the template.

SHOP TIP

Copying a leg
In cases where it is not possible to set an existing leg on a template, as shown on page 76, use a compass and a piece of white paper taped to a board to help you draw the leg's contours. For a table leg, clamp the board to the rail so the paper will sit alongside the leg. Then, holding the compass level, ride the pivot point along one edge of the leg; the pencil point will simultaneously mark the profile on the paper. Repeat for the other edge of the leg.

RETIPPING A DAMAGED LEG

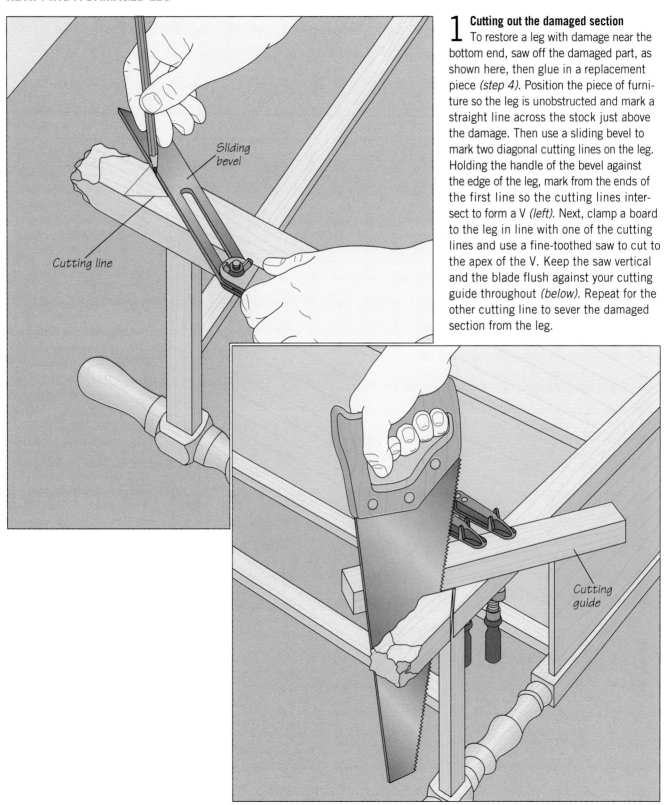

1 Cutting out the damaged section

To restore a leg with damage near the bottom end, saw off the damaged part, as shown here, then glue in a replacement piece *(step 4)*. Position the piece of furniture so the leg is unobstructed and mark a straight line across the stock just above the damage. Then use a sliding bevel to mark two diagonal cutting lines on the leg. Holding the handle of the bevel against the edge of the leg, mark from the ends of the first line so the cutting lines intersect to form a V *(left)*. Next, clamp a board to the leg in line with one of the cutting lines and use a fine-toothed saw to cut to the apex of the V. Keep the saw vertical and the blade flush against your cutting guide throughout *(below)*. Repeat for the other cutting line to sever the damaged section from the leg.

Sliding bevel

Cutting line

Cutting guide

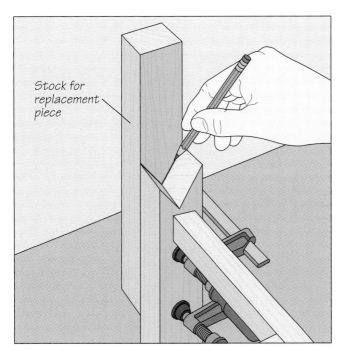

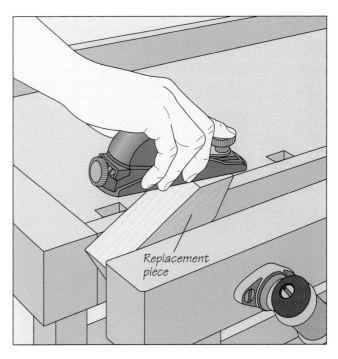

2 Outlining the replacement piece

Cut the replacement piece from a wood species that matches the leg's grain and color as closely as possible. Cut the board to the same width and thickness as the leg, then clamp it to the leg so the pieces are face-to-face and the new tip extends beyond the V by an amount equal to the section you removed, plus about 1 inch. Outline the V on the replacement piece with a pencil *(above)*.

3 Preparing the replacement piece

Cut the end of the replacement piece with a backsaw, following the lines you marked in step 2. Test-fit the piece in the V you cut in the leg; the pieces should fit together snugly. To fine-tune the fit, secure the replacement piece in a bench vise and use a block plane to trim it *(above)*. Make adjustments to the new piece, rather than the leg.

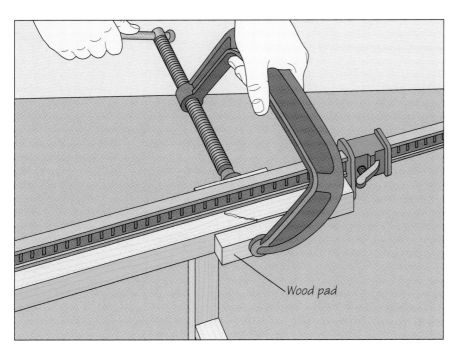

4 Gluing the replacement to the leg

Spread glue on the contacting surfaces between the leg and the replacement piece, fit them together, and secure the joint with a bar clamp. To prevent the pieces from sliding out of alignment, install a clamp on the edges of the leg, centering the jaws on the joint and spreading the pressure with wood pads *(left)*. Once the adhesive has cured, trim the leg to length and sand the surface smooth.

REPLACING MOLDING

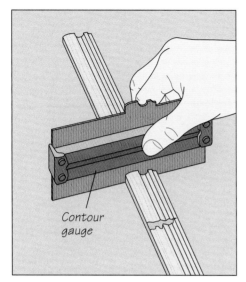

Contour gauge

1 Copying the molding profile

To make replacement molding, you can use a contour gauge to copy the profile of the damaged piece. Carefully remove the molding from the furniture and place it contoured-side up on a work surface. Holding the gauge perpendicular to the molding, press it against the surface *(above)*. The tightly packed, retractable steel needles will mirror the molding profile, enabling you to choose the right combination of table saw molding cutters and router bits to shape the replacement piece.

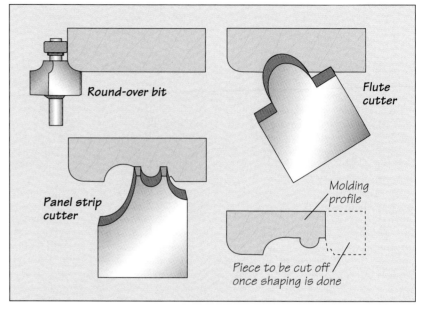

Round-over bit

Flute cutter

Panel strip cutter

Molding profile

Piece to be cut off once shaping is done

2 Planning the cuts

Outline the molding profile on a piece of paper, using the contour gauge as a guide. Then refer to your drawing to select the molding cutters and bits you will need to replicate the profile. For the molding shown in the bottom right-hand corner of the illustration above (and in the color photograph on page 74), you would use a table-mounted router to round over the edge *(step 3)*, then make two passes on the table saw with different cutters to complete the piece *(step 4)*. Because it is safer to shape a wider board, cut the excess wood from the straight edge once you have finished shaping the workpiece. The illustration below shows a variety of router bits and the profiles they cut in wood, and a selection of table saw molding cutters.

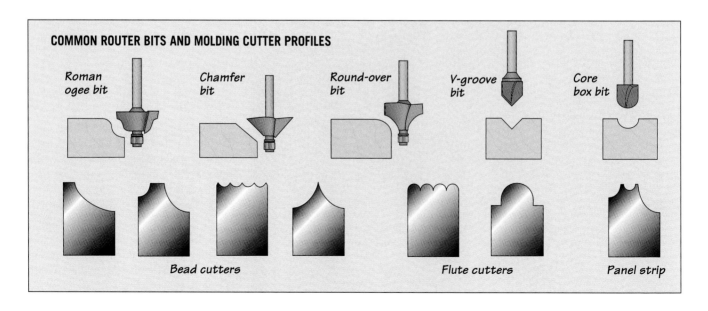

COMMON ROUTER BITS AND MOLDING CUTTER PROFILES

Roman ogee bit

Chamfer bit

Round-over bit

V-groove bit

Core box bit

Bead cutters

Flute cutters

Panel strip

3 Rounding over the molding

Install a round-over bit in a router and mount the tool in a table. Position the fence for the appropriate cutting width and adjust the height. Use three featherboards to support the workpiece, clamping two to the fence, one on each side of the bit, and a third to the table in line with the cutter; brace this featherboard with a support board. (In the illustration at right, the featherboard on the outfeed side of the fence has been removed for clarity.) Feed the workpiece slowly past the bit, keeping it pressed against the fence. Finish the pass with a push stick.

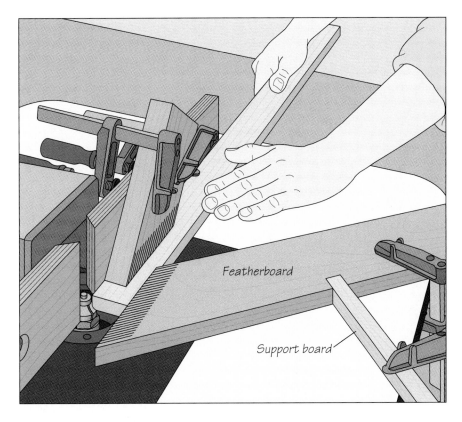

Featherboard

Support board

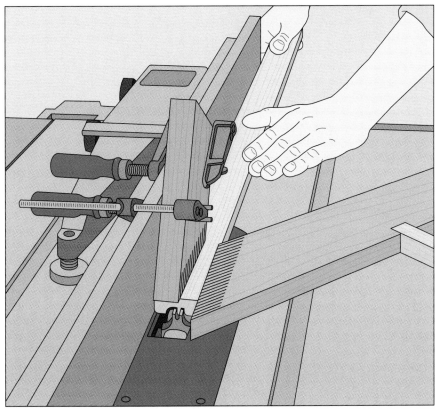

4 Shaping the molding on the table saw

Mount the flute cutters in your table saw's molding head and install the head on the arbor. Angle the head as necessary and set the cutting height at ⅛ inch. Position the workpiece over the cutter, then butt the fence against the stock and lock it in place. For this operation, use two featherboards to brace the workpiece, clamping one to the fence and one to the table. Feed the molding across the table, finishing the pass with a push stick. Repeat, making as many passes as necessary to deepen the cut and raising the cutters by ⅛ inch per pass. Once you are satisfied with the profile, repeat the process with the panel strip cutters *(left)*. Install a combination blade on the saw to rip the molding to width.

A COVE-CUTTING GUIDE

You can fashion coved molding on your table saw using the jig shown at right. To build the guide, fasten two 18-inch-long 1-by-2s to two 9-inch-long 1-by-2s with carriage bolts and wing nuts, forming two sets of parallel arms. Adjust the jig so the distance between the inside edges of the two long arms equals the width of the cove you wish to produce. Set the cutting height, then lay the guide across the blade and rotate it until the blade, turned by hand, just touches the inside edges of the long arms. Run a pencil along the inside edges of the arms to mark guidelines across the table insert *(right, middle)*. Remove the jig and lower the blade beneath the table. Outline the cove you wish to cut on the leading end of the workpiece, then set the stock on the saw table, aligning the marked outline with the guidelines on the table insert. Butt guide boards against the edges of the workpiece and clamp them in place parallel to the guidelines; the boards should be long enough to span the saw table. Set a cutting height of 1/8 inch, then make the first pass, feeding the workpiece steadily *(right, bottom)*; use push blocks when your hands approach the blade. Make as many passes as necessary, raising the blade 1/8 inch at a time.

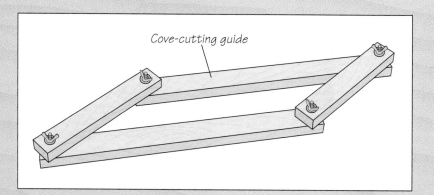

Cove-cutting guide

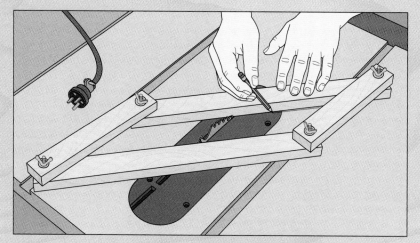

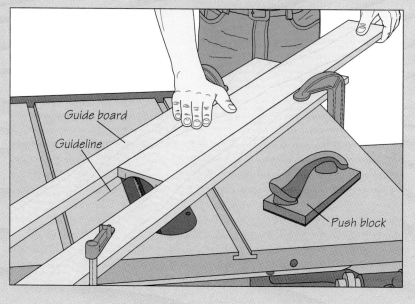

Guide board

Guideline

Push block

A ny antique that has led a full life almost certainly will show evidence of it. Your first task in evaluating flaws such as broken corners and chipped edges is to determine whether they contribute to the character of a piece—and should be left alone—or whether they must be fixed. Consider the seriousness of the flaw as well as your ability to make the repair appear unobtrusive.

A tabletop with a broken corner is a typical blemish you might find on an antique. Repairing a top can be a tricky undertaking because it is a table's most visible surface. If the damage is slight and only bears witness to the table's age, it should probably not be touched. But if the broken corner reveals a jagged edge, ruining the table's lines, you should attempt a repair.

Exercise the same caution when considering the possibility of filling a surface flaw with a wood plug. Some faults are best left alone, for they can give furniture a look of distinguished experience. Others, such as empty screw holes, that indicate an earlier, botched repair ought to be concealed. As shown in the color photo on page 88, install a plug that is as invisible as possible.

Depending on the severity and location of the problem, there are different ways to repair damaged surfaces and edges. The following pages show a variety of seamless fixes for timeworn antiques. Keep in mind that you still have work to do after grafting a replacement piece onto an antique. Refer to the Restoration Basics chapter *(page 12)* for ways of treating new wood so it will blend into its surroundings.

A missing section from the table leg shown above has been replaced with a snug-fitting wood block. After being glued in place, the graft was shaped to match the leg's contours, as shown on page 87. A matching stain and finish will be applied next.

REPAIRING A DAMAGED CORNER

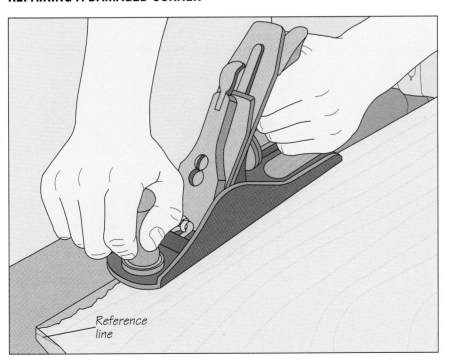

Reference line

1 Preparing the surface
Before you can graft a piece of new wood onto a damaged corner, as on the tabletop shown at left, the affected area must be perfectly flat. Start by using a rule to mark a reference line along the edge and end of the workpiece to define the damaged area. Then use a bench plane adjusted to a very light cut to flatten the area. Keep the blade within your reference line, working carefully to avoid removing wood from the undamaged section.

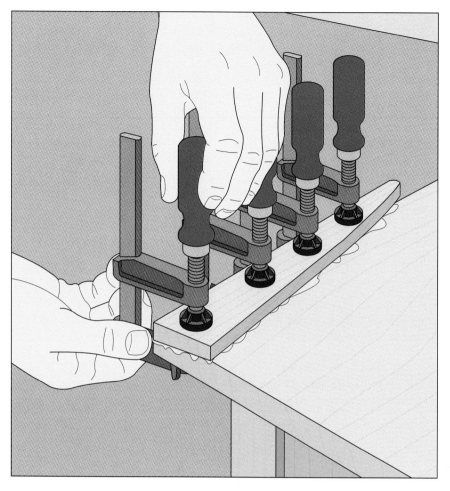

2 Gluing down the replacement piece
Cut a piece of wood that matches the grain and color of the tabletop as closely as possible. Although the top face and edges of the piece can extend beyond the repair area, make sure that the ends are flush with the table. Because they are long-grain surfaces, the top and edges of the piece can easily be smoothed down with a plane; however, it is difficult to plane end grain without some unsightly tearout. Test-fit the graft in position, trim it if necessary, then spread glue on its bottom face and on the tabletop's repair area. Secure the graft in place *(left)*, spacing the clamps about 3 to 4 inches apart.

3 Smoothing the repair
Once the glue has cured, use the bench plane to cut down the outside edge and top face of the graft until it is flush with the tabletop *(below)*. As a guide, mark the edge of the tabletop on the outside edge of the new piece and plane the top surface until you reach the line. To avoid tearout, work with the wood grain throughout. To complete the repair, sand the area flush with the surrounding wood.

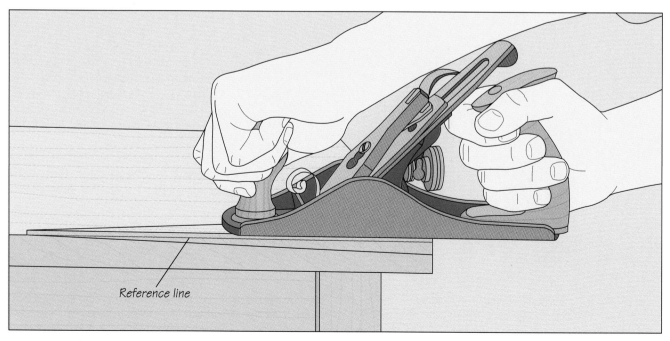

Reference line

BUILDING UP THE EDGE OF A DECORATED SURFACE

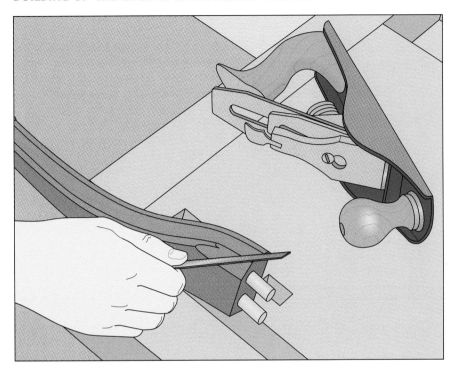

1 Preparing the damaged surface
To repair a chipped edge with a new piece of wood, start by squaring up the damaged area. Secure the workpiece in a bench vise, then use a bench plane adjusted to a very light cut to flatten the surface, checking with a rule on edge to ensure that the area is square and even *(left)*. Work carefully and slowly to avoid removing too much wood.

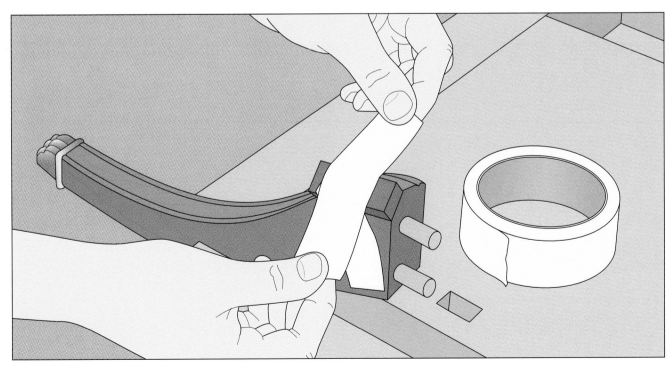

2 Gluing down the graft
Cut a piece of wood to the same length and width as the prepared surface, using a species that closely matches the grain and color of the workpiece. The graft can be thicker than you need, since you will be sanding it down in step 3. Spread glue on the contacting surfaces between the graft and the workpiece and clamp them together with masking tape.

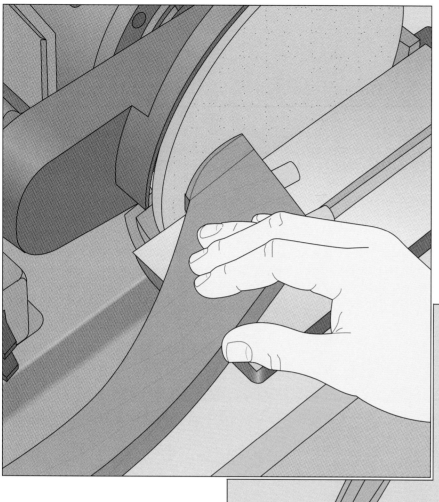

3 Trimming and sanding the graft to size
Once the glue has cured, trim the graft to size on your band saw. To replicate any curved contours on the surface of the graft, use a disk sander, as shown at left, a spindle sander, or a sanding block. For the disk sander, hold the workpiece flat on the sanding table and guide the graft across the spinning disk. Continue until the curves on the graft match those of the workpiece.

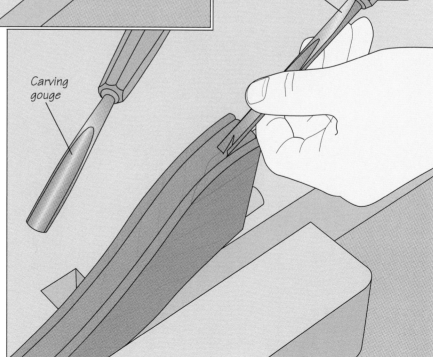

V-gouge

Carving
gouge

4 Shaping the graft
For a workpiece with decorative elements such as the cabriole leg shown in this section, secure the stock in a bench vise and use carving tools to do the required shaping. To carve a bead, for example, start with a round carving gouge to round over the edge of the surface, then cut the bead with a V-gouge *(right)*. Always follow the grain of the wood to avoid gouging the stock. Finish shaping the surface with sandpaper.

BUILDING UP THE EDGE OF A CONTOURED SURFACE

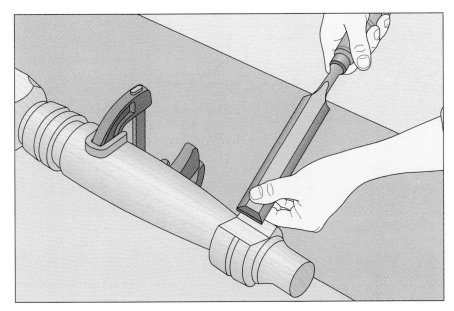

1 Preparing the damaged area
For a turned leg like the one shown at left, prepare a chipped edge for a graft by cutting an angled notch. The graft will be cut to fit in the notch. Clamp the leg to a work surface, then use a chisel with the bevel side up to pare away thin shavings to create the two flat sides of the notch. Cut away as little wood as possible.

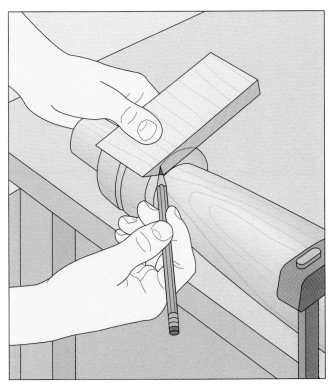

2 Gluing down the replacement block
To prepare the graft, cut its bottom surface with the chisel to fit snugly in the leg notch. Then holding the piece in position in the notch, trace the contour of the leg surface on one edge *(above)*. Trim the graft to size on your band saw, then glue and clamp it in place.

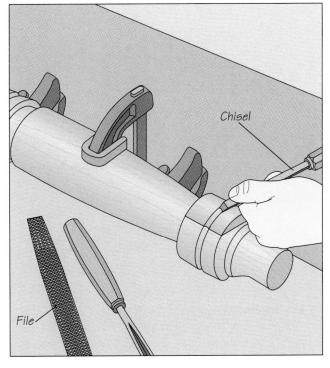

3 Shaping the block
Use a rasp to remove any marks from the graft left by the band saw blade and to shape its surface to conform to the contours of the leg. If the leg features decorative elements, such as a bead, use a V-gouge and a chisel to carve it into the graft *(above)*. Smooth the surface with a file and then sand it with progressively finer grits.

FILLING SURFACE DAMAGE WITH WOOD PLUGS

1 Preparing the surface for a plug
An effective way to repair deep surface defects like screw holes or burns is to fill the damage with a wood plug. Start by drilling a hole into the surface to accept the plug. Fit an electric drill with a brad-point or Forstner bit slightly larger than the defect, center the bit over the damage, and bore a ½-inch-deep hole. Keep the drill vertical throughout *(right)* and avoid boring completely through the workpiece.

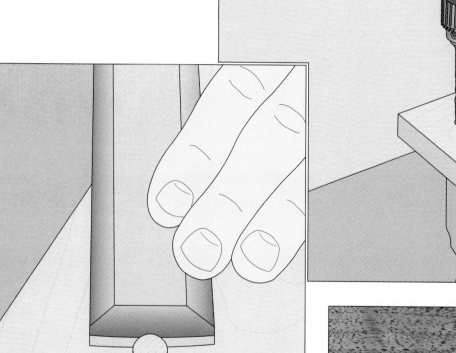

2 Inserting the plug
To ensure that the plug blends with the color and grain of the surface, make your own from a matching piece of wood. Using a plug cutter on your drill press, cut several plugs from the face of the board, making sure their diameter is identical to that of the hole you drilled in step 1. The plugs should be slightly longer than the depth of the hole. Compare each plug with the surface and choose the one that blends in best. Spread glue on the plug and in the hole, insert the plug, and tap it in place with a mallet. Trim the plug flush with the surface using a chisel *(above)*, then sand the surface smooth.

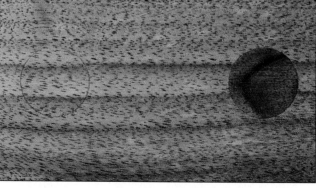

Making an invisible repair with a wood plug depends on how well its color and grain resembles the surrounding wood. The plug on the left in the photo above is an almost perfect match. The one on the right stands out because of its contrasting color and grain. Both plugs came from the same board.

REPAIRING VENEER

The practice of covering relatively inexpensive or nondescript-looking woods with thin sheets of beautiful or rare species has offered benefits to cabinetmakers for centuries—and continues to do so. Besides the obvious cost savings, the flexibility of veneer allows a wood's grain and figure to be carried around a contoured surface—a feat often impossible to achieve with solid stock. In addition, veneer can be glued onto fiberboard or plywood, taking advantage of these materials' resistance to wood movement.

But using veneer does eventually carry a price. Over time, the sheet tends to separate from the substrate, developing blisters, air bubbles, and cracks. Pieces with solid-wood substrates that have different shrinkage characteristics than the veneer are particularly vulnerable to these problems. Two techniques for repairing blisters are explained starting on page 92.

As shown below and on page 90, there are two time-honored methods for replacing damaged veneer. A veneer punch will cut a piece of veneer from the surface and then an identical patch from a replacement sheet. Since the punch cuts an irregular shape, it offers

the best method for repairing figured woods like bird's-eye maple burl. For straight-grained species, the diamond patch method is adequate.

Until the turn of the century, veneer was plain-sawn from logs in thicknesses of at least 1/16 inch. In fact, the thickness of veneer is often a good indication of an antique's age. The thicker the veneer, the older the antique. Today, most veneer is peeled from logs on a type of giant lathe, producing paper-thin sheets. If you are replacing thicker, plain-sawn veneer, be sure to use the same type.

A strip of veneer is being glued down to fill a gap on the top of a 19th Century grandfather clock. Because breaks in veneer are often jagged, it is important to cut the edges of the damaged area straight before preparing the patch to ensure a seamless repair.

USING A VENEER PUNCH

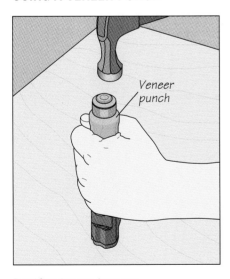

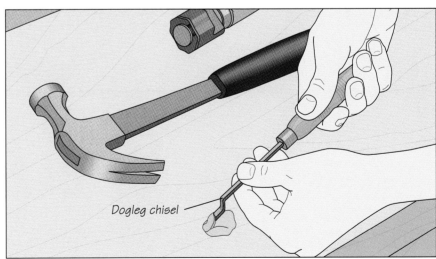

Patching damaged veneer

You can repair a small section of damaged veneer by cutting it out with a veneer punch and replacing the piece with a patch of matching veneer. On an older piece of furniture, the veneer is most likely to have been bonded to the substrate with hide glue. To soften the adhesive, heat the damaged area with an iron before using the punch. To remove the damaged section, position the punch with the tool's cutting edge flat on the veneer. Strike the punch sharply with a hammer *(above, left)*. If the veneer does not come off in the punch, use a dogleg chisel to pare it away, being careful not to gouge the substrate panel *(above, right)*. Next, punch out a piece of veneer to replace the damaged section, being sure to match the grain of the removed piece as closely as possible. Glue the patch in place *(page 91)*.

REPLACING DAMAGED VENEER WITH A DIAMOND PATCH

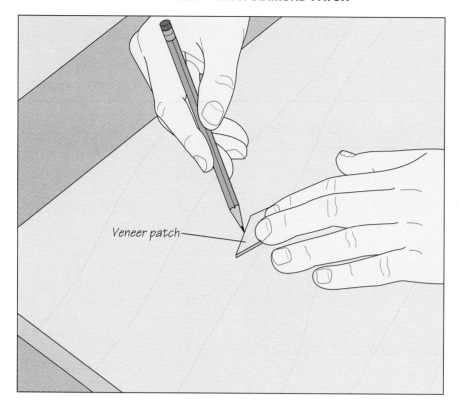

Veneer patch

1 Outlining the patch on the surface
The veneer-repairing method shown on this page involves cutting a patch first, and then gluing it into a matching recess on the surface. Using a craft knife, cut the patch in a diamond shape, which will be less conspicuous than a rectangular piece. For a tighter fit, bevel the undersides of the patch, making sure it is slightly larger than the damaged area. Then position the patch over the surface so its grain pattern runs in the same direction and outline its profile with a sharp pencil *(left)*.

2 Cutting the recess for the patch
Aligning a hardwood board or a straightedge as a guide, cut just to the waste side of your cutting lines with the craft knife *(right)*. Slice the surface to a depth equal to the thickness of the patch. Then clean out the recess using a dogleg chisel or a paring chisel.

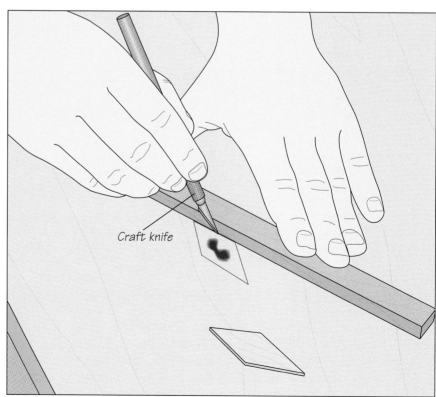

Craft knife

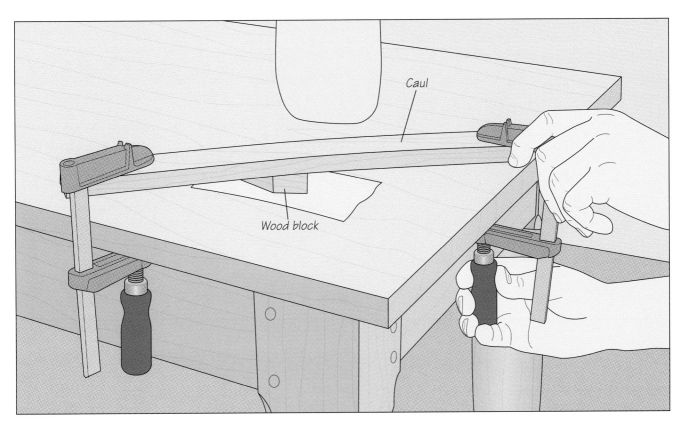

Caul

Wood block

SHOP TIP

Extracting grit from under veneer
Specks of dirt or dust trapped under a sheet of veneer can cause it to lift off the substrate panel. To smooth out these lumps, use a craft knife to make an angled incision around the problem area. Then peel back the flap of veneer *(right)* and use the knife to extract the foreign body. (A cut made with the grain will help make the repair less visible.) Next, refasten the flap to the substrate. If the veneer was attached using hide glue, follow the fastening technique shown in the Shop Tip on page 93. With other adhesives, apply a dab of glue to the substrate and the underside of the flap and clamp it down, as shown above.

3 Gluing down the patch
Spread glue in the recess and set the patch in place, then secure it with a wood block and two clamps. Lay a piece of wax paper over the patch and hold it down with the clamps. If the block is farther from the edges of the surface than the clamps can reach, use a wood caul as a clamp extension. Place the caul on the wood block, install a clamp at each end, and tighten the clamps until the caul is holding the block tightly in place *(above)*. Work quickly to prevent the patch from absorbing moisture from the adhesive and swelling. Once the glue has cured, remove the clamping setup and sand the patch flush with the surface, working carefully to avoid marring the original finish.

FIXING BLISTERED VENEER

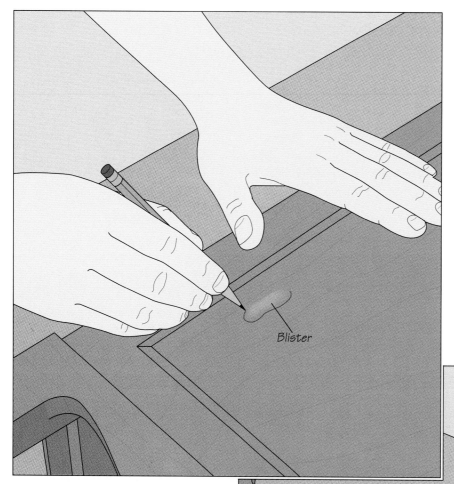

Blister

1 Outlining the blister
To repair a blister in veneer, try the method described in the Shop Tip on page 93. If this does not work, you will have to slice open the blister, as shown below, inject some glue into it *(step 3)*, and clamp it down *(step 4)*. Start by finding the edges of the blister by tapping around it with a fingernail; the blistered section will produce a hollow sound. Once you have determined the extend of the damage, lightly mark its outline on the surface with a pencil *(left)*.

2 Slicing the blister open
Cutting with the grain of the veneer, slice open the blister with a craft knife *(right)*. Keep the cut within the blister's outline. To remove debris from under the blister, press down on one side of the flap and use the knife to scrape out old glue and foreign particles from under the adjacent flap. Repeat on the other side of the blister.

Craft knife

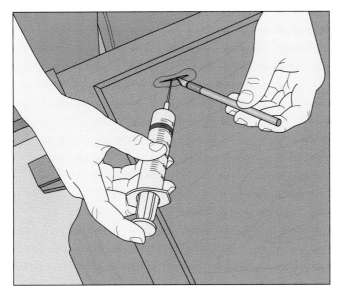

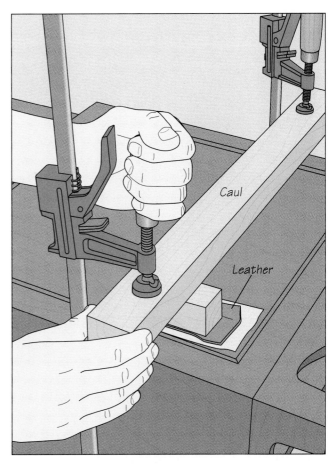

Caul

Leather

3 Injecting glue under the blister
To refasten the blistered veneer to the substrate, use the craft knife to gently pry open one of the flaps and squirt in some adhesive with a syringe-style glue injector *(above)*. Repeat for the other flap. Apply gentle pressure with the knife to avoid marring the surface. If you do not have a glue injector, you can apply the adhesive with a finishing nail. For a large blister, the curved, flexible blade of a grapefruit knife works well for spreading glue under the blister. Wipe away any excess glue with a dampened cloth.

4 Securing the veneer
Secure the blister with a clamping arrangement similar to the setup shown on page 91. In this repair, a piece of leather is sandwiched between the wax paper and the wood block to protect the surface, and quick-action bar clamps are used instead of C clamps to account for the thickness of the surface *(above)*.

SHOP TIP

Refastening hide-glued veneer
On most antiques, veneers are bonded with hide glue. One advantage of this adhesive is that heat can reactivate the glue. To flatten a blister in hide-glued veneer, place a slightly dampened cloth on the affected area and pass a household iron set to moderate heat over the material *(right)*. In a few minutes, the glue should soften and the pressure applied by the iron should smooth out the blister. Once the blister is flat, clamp the veneer as described above.

SURFACE AND FINISH REPAIRS

A wad of fine steel wool wrapped around the end of a dowel rubs a stain out of a tabletop. Using the dowel concentrates the abrasive action on the blemish, minimizing damage to the surrounding finish.

Once all of the structural repairs have been completed, you should direct your attention to the finish of your antique. Chances are, furniture with loose joints or surface cracks will also have a damaged finish. The flaws can range from relatively superficial blemishes, such as stains, dents, and nicks, to more serious problems, including widespread cracking or flaking of the surface.

A common misconception among amateur restorers is that a flawed finish must be stripped off completely and a new finish applied. But in fact, the finish on many older pieces is salvageable, provided the surface coating is basically sound and the damage is confined to an area you can reasonably repair. Stripping and refinishing should be a last resort. There are three principal advantages to simple repair. You will minimize your exposure to toxic chemical strippers, spare yourself considerable time and expense, and you will maintain the value and appearance of the antique by preserving as much of the original finish as possible.

As a first step, clean the surface of the piece thoroughly, as described in the Restoring Basics chapter *(page 17)*, then determine the condition of the finish *(page 96)*. This will tell you whether the topcoat is damaged beyond repair and must be stripped *(page 110)* or whether it is sound and can be saved. All of the finish repairs presented in this chapter are easy to do, and the tools and materials required are readily available. In many cases, particularly if the fix involves the use of a solvent or filler, you will need to identify the type of finish on the piece *(page 96)*. This will ensure that the product you use will be compatible with the existing finish.

Your choice of the appropriate repair strategy and materials for a particular blemish will depend on the nature of the damage. Stains and water rings can usually be rubbed away *(page 99)*. A suitable repair for a dent, for example, is to raise it with steam *(page 105)*. However, if the wood fibers beneath the finish are severed rather than simply crushed, steam will not work; a wood filler *(page 102)* may be the best remedy. For small flaws, wax or shellac sticks can produce a virtually invisible fix. Both are available in a variety of colors to match many wood species.

Many larger blemishes are best concealed using a wood filler. Although many fillers are pre-colored, you can tint filler yourself for a perfect match. Test the filler on an inconspicuous spot of the workpiece before committing yourself to a particular formula.

A traditional shellac stick is one of the best methods for repairing minor damage to a finish. Heated by the flame from an alcohol lamp, a burn-in knife melts a small bit of the shellac stick to fill the hole. When the shellac cools, it is leveled with a felt block.

IDENTIFYING FINISHES

Once you have ascertained that a finish needs repairing (*photo, below*), you need to establish the type of finish you have, for unless you use a product that is identical to or compatible with the original finish, the product may dissolve the finish surrounding the blemish, rather than simply blending with it and covering the area.

There are several ways to determine the type of finish on an antique, some more precise than others. The appearance of the finish can be a reliable guide. Different products, such as penetrating oils, shellac, or varnish, have unique characteristics, and a practised eye can often distinguish one from another. The chart below describes the finishes commonly found on antiques.

The age of a piece can also be a clue to the finish applied to it. Most furniture dating from the 18th Century, for example, will likely have been finished with a wax or penetrating oil. By the 19th Century, shellac was the finish of choice for high-quality furniture. Any piece built after 1900 may have been finished with either lacquer, varnish, or polyurethane.

As shown on page 97, the most reliable method of identifying a finish is to try to dissolve a small section of it using a solvent. If you use this technique, it is important to apply the appropriate solvents in the correct sequence. Start with turpentine, since it dissolves only wax-based finishes. If it has no effect, move on to denatured alcohol, which will also dissolve shellac. If the finish remains intact, try lacquer thinner; it dissolves shellac and lacquer. If the finish still has not dissolved, apply methylene chloride, which will work on all of the preceding finishes as well as varnish and polyurethane. A finish that resists all these solvents is most likely a penetrating oil.

The bottom of a spoon is run along the top of a desk, testing whether the finish is salvageable. If the spoon leaves no trace or makes only a powdery whitish mark, the finish is sound. However, if the finish flakes off or cracks under moderate pressure, it will have to be stripped off.

CHARACTERISTICS OF WOOD FINISHES

TYPE	CHARACTERISTICS
Wax	Produces a bright shine when buffed. Usually applied over a penetrating oil finish to protect it. Must be cleaned and buffed regularly and reapplied periodically. Available in liquid and paste form.
Penetrating oil	Produces a soft, flat luster, which deepens with additional coats. Less durable than other finishes, but will not chip or peel. Low resistance to water and alcohol; usually waxed. Very easy to apply. Available in liquid form.
Shellac	Produces a glossy, clear finish, which darkens to an amber color over time. Susceptible to heat, water and alcohol damage; moisture present during application produces a blemish known as blushing, a white haze on the surface. Available in solid flake or liquid form.
Lacquer	Produces a hard, abrasion-resistant and clear finish. Has excellent resistance to heat and moisture. Dries quickly and can be applied in several coats in one day. Due to its extremely fast drying time, this liquid is often sprayed onto the surface but can be brushed on if a retarder is added to slow the drying time.
Varnish	Produces a bright, glossy shine that highlights the wood's grain pattern. Available in three different liquid formulations: long, medium and short oil, which differ in durability and gloss. Long-oil is the most durable, but takes a longer time to dry, allowing dust to settle on the finish while it is tacky.
Polyurethane	Ranges from a bright glossy shine to a smooth mellow sheen. Extremely durable and will not darken with age. Highly resistant to water and alcohol damage. Difficult to strip off if repairs are necessary. Easy to apply with brush or by spraying; fast drying.

IDENTIFYING A FINISH

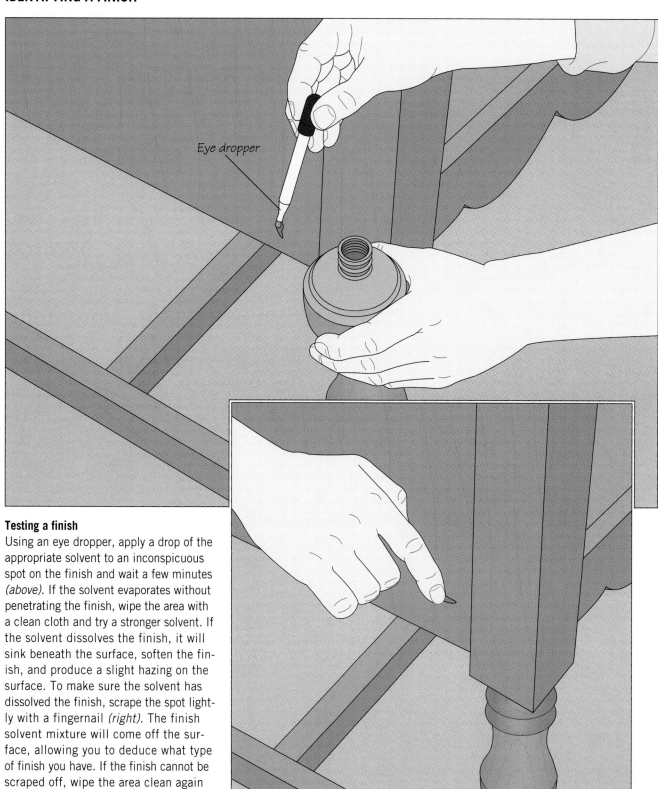

Eye dropper

Testing a finish
Using an eye dropper, apply a drop of the appropriate solvent to an inconspicuous spot on the finish and wait a few minutes *(above)*. If the solvent evaporates without penetrating the finish, wipe the area with a clean cloth and try a stronger solvent. If the solvent dissolves the finish, it will sink beneath the surface, soften the finish, and produce a slight hazing on the surface. To make sure the solvent has dissolved the finish, scrape the spot lightly with a fingernail *(right)*. The finish solvent mixture will come off the surface, allowing you to deduce what type of finish you have. If the finish cannot be scraped off, wipe the area clean again and try a stronger solvent.

REPAIRING SURFACES AND FINISHES

This section presents a variety of repairs you can undertake to fix damaged surfaces and finishes. The chart below lists the problems most commonly found on antiques and suggests remedies for each. Start with the least damaging or invasive procedure and only progress to a more aggressive method if necessary. To rub away a stain *(page 99)*, for example, start with a cloth dampened with water. If this fails, try naphtha (lighter fluid). Only move on to an abrasive, such as fine sandpaper or rottenstone, after a gentler approach has had no effect.

Touch-up kits, like the one shown at right, feature a complete array of supplies for surface and finish repairs. The commercial kit shown includes tools, such as artists' brushes and fine steel wool, and materials like wax sticks, powdered stains that match various wood species, epoxy, polish, and leveling solution.

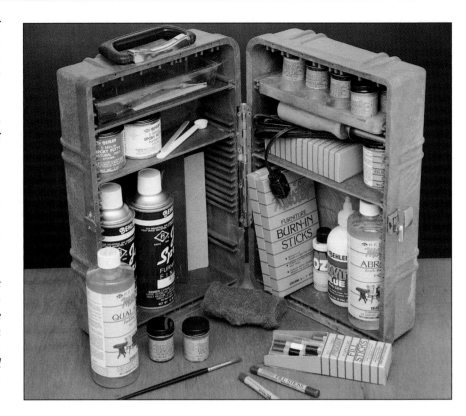

SURFACE BLEMISHES AND REMEDIES

BLEMISH	REMEDY
Stain	Try rubbing a stain away *(page 99)*, beginning with the mildest cleaning agent and progressing to more aggressive cleaners or abrasives as necessary. A typical progression would be: water; naphtha; cigarette ashes mixed with a light lubricant, like mineral oil; table salt; rottenstone and mineral oil; pumice and mineral oil; a commercial spot-removing product.
Burn	Scrape the burn with the edge of a sharp razor blade *(page 100)*. Remove all traces of the scrapings with a toothbrush, and bleach the tarnished area with a cotton swab dipped in denatured alcohol. Fill any small depression with a wood-patching compound *(page 102)*.
Dent	Try lifting the dent with steam *(page 105)*; if steam does not work, fill the dent.
Scratch	Using 4/0 steel wool and the appropriate solvent for the finish *(page 96)*, dissolve some of the finish surrounding the scratch, and allow it to flow into the scratch to fill it. Scratches can also be repaired with a wood-patching compound *(page 102)*.
Hole	Fill with a wood-patching compound *(page 102)*.
Gouge	Fill with a wood-patching compound *(page 102)*.
Water ring	Rub away with an abrasive *(page 101)*.
Damaged corner or edge	Rebuild with a solid patch *(page 102)* or with a filler *(page 106)*.
"Alligatored" finish	An alligatored finish—one with a widespread pattern of cracks on the surface—should be stripped off *(page 110)*.
Foggy finish	Strip off the finish *(page 110)*.

REMOVING A STAIN

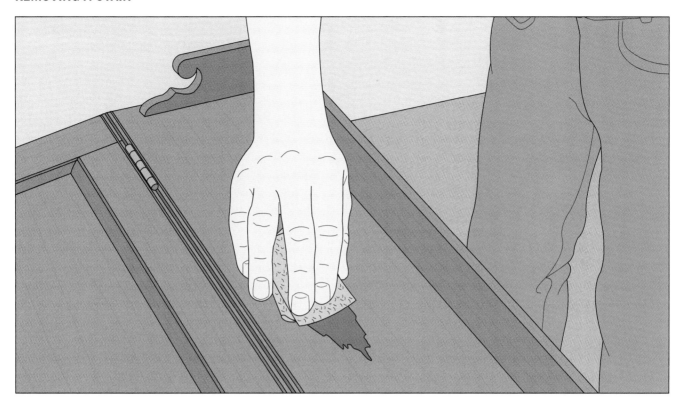

1 Rubbing away a stain
Inspect the stain to determine how far into the finish it penetrates. If the blemish obscures the surface gloss on the workpiece, it is probably confined to the finish and can be rubbed away. If not, the stain is beneath the finish and on the wood surface; in this case, you may wish to consult a professional. To remove a stain from the finish, dampen a cloth with water and rub the affected area with a back-and-forth motion. If the stain remains, repeat the procedure, using progressively more aggressive cleaning agents and abrasives, as suggested in the chart on page 98. If you use fine sandpaper *(above)* or rottenstone or pumice, always work with the wood grain.

SHOP TIP

Removing excess stain or finish from a brush
Whether you are applying a stain or a finish, the best implement for making a spot-repair is an artist's brush. However, simply dipping the brush into your solution and applying it to a small scratch or spot may cause the liquid to pool on the surface and overrun the affected area; you may end up with a more unsightly blemish than the one you repaired. To remove excess liquid from a brush, stroke the bristles across strips of masking tape, as shown at right. The tape will leave just the right amount of liquid on the brush, allowing you to apply a thin and controlled coat.

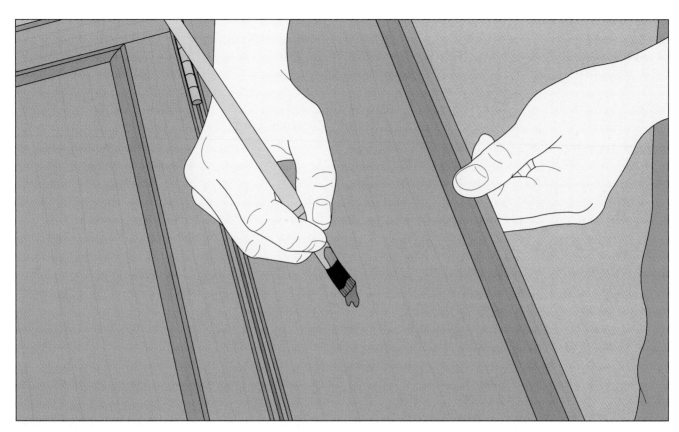

2 Refinishing a spot-repair

Once you have removed a blemish from the surface, you will need to stain the affected spot to match the surrounding area *(page 121)*, if necessary, and then apply a new finish. Use an artist's brush—either a narrow flat-head type, as shown above, or a fine-point sable type—to stain or finish a small area. Brush the liquid sparingly in as thin a coat as possible, working with the grain and avoiding the surrounding finish as much as possible. Let the liquid dry. Apply as many coats of finish as necessary until the affected area is level with the surrounding finish.

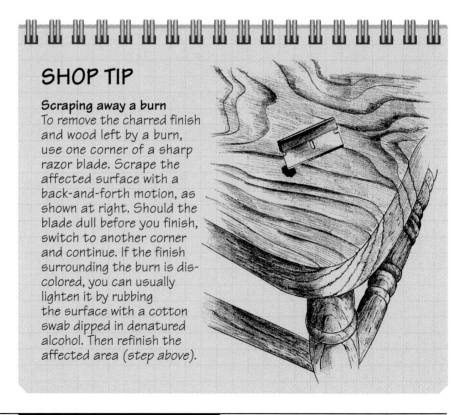

SHOP TIP

Scraping away a burn
To remove the charred finish and wood left by a burn, use one corner of a sharp razor blade. Scrape the affected surface with a back-and-forth motion, as shown at right. Should the blade dull before you finish, switch to another corner and continue. If the finish surrounding the burn is discolored, you can usually lighten it by rubbing the surface with a cotton swab dipped in denatured alcohol. Then refinish the affected area *(step above)*.

REMOVING A WATER RING

1 Using steel wool
Water rings usually appear as white circles on the finish. Try rubbing the affected area with 4/0 steel wool. Always work in the direction of the wood grain, avoiding the surrounding surface as much as possible *(right)*. If the water ring remains after a reasonable amount of time, try a more aggressive abrasive *(step 2)*.

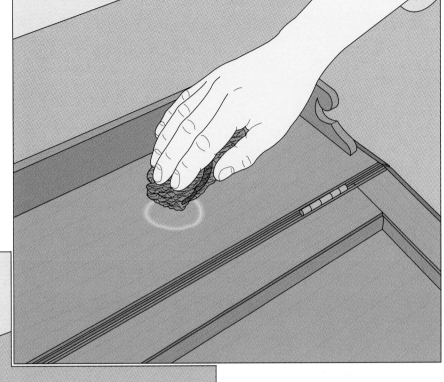

2 Using rottenstone
To remove a stubborn water ring, use rottenstone—a fine abrasive powder made from pulverized limestone. Sprinkle a little rottenstone on the affected area and gently rub the surface with a cheesecloth pad, working in the direction of the grain *(left)*. Avoid abrading the surrounding finish as much as possible. If the ring remains, repeat the process, applying a few drops of mineral spirits as a lubricant. The rottenstone and mineral spirits will produce an abrasive slurry that should eventually eliminate the water ring. Once the blemish is gone, refinish the affected area *(page 100)*.

WOOD-PATCHING COMPOUNDS

TYPE	CHARACTERISTICS	USES	COMPATIBILITIES
Wood filler	Solvent- or water-based; depending on type, can be tinted with stain or purchased pre-tinted	Filling large holes, gouges, cracks and dents; two-part epoxy type ideal for contoured surfaces	Compatible with most finishes; apply before or after stain
Wax stick	Wax- and resin-based; available in a variety of colors. Sets quickly	Filling small holes, scratches, and cracks	May be incompatible with lacquer; apply after finishing
Shellac stick	Shellac- and resin-based; available in a variety of colors. Sets quickly to form a hard surface	Filling scratches, dents, and gouges	May not be compatible with alcohol- or lacquer-based finishes; apply before or after finishing
Shop-made filler	Sawdust mixed with binder, such as hide glue or shellac; can be tinted with stain	Filling narrow cracks, gaps, and small holes	Compatible with most finishes

Most modern patching compounds are formulated to be chemically compatible with a variety of finishes, but in cases where the two products contain the same solvent, the finish can dissolve the filler. Use the chart above to choose the appropriate patching compound for the type of finish you intend to apply.

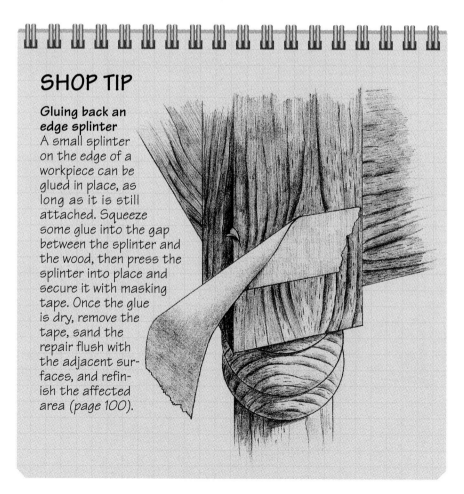

SHOP TIP

Gluing back an edge splinter
A small splinter on the edge of a workpiece can be glued in place, as long as it is still attached. Squeeze some glue into the gap between the splinter and the wood, then press the splinter into place and secure it with masking tape. Once the glue is dry, remove the tape, sand the repair flush with the adjacent surfaces, and refinish the affected area (page 100).

REPAIRING SCRATCHES

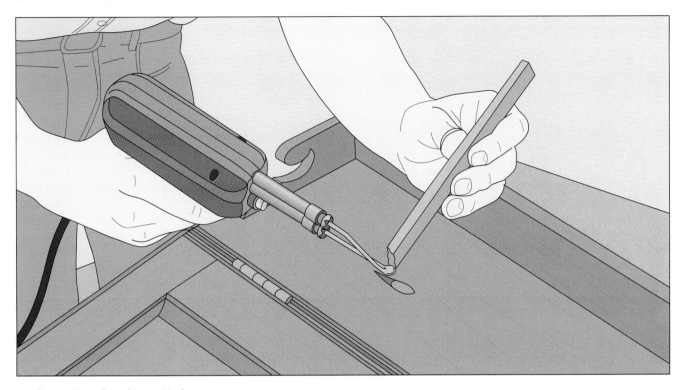

Melting shellac stick with a soldering gun

Select a shellac stick of the appropriate color and turn on a soldering gun. To avoid transferring dirt or foreign particles to your repair, clean the tip of the gun with steel wool. Then, holding the shellac stick over the hole, melt it with the tip of the gun *(above)*. Be careful not to blacken the shellac. If it does darken, remove the gun, cut off the blackened portion, and try again. Melt enough of the product to fill the hole. While the filler is still soft, use a knife or a chisel to press it evenly into the damaged area. Work carefully to avoid marring the surrounding area. Once the filler is cool, level it *(page 104)*.

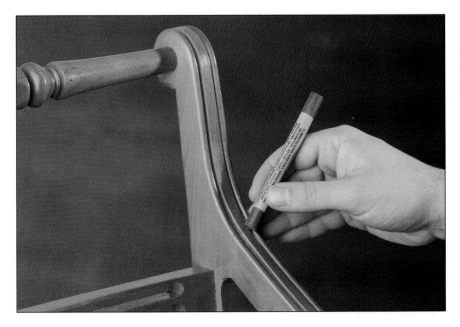

A wax crayon is rubbed back and forth along an arm of the chair shown at left, filling a small scratch. For best results, work the crayon in the direction of the wood grain. Once the flaw is level with the surrounding surface, you can simply wipe off the excess with a clean pad or cloth. Since some types of wax crayons are incompatible with lacquer, you should refinish the damage (page 100) *before using the crayon if you are planning to apply lacquer. Otherwise, the lacquer may dissolve the wax. Wax crayons are excellent for small scratches and cracks; for a larger scratch, dent, or gouge, try melting shellac stick to fill the blemish, as shown above and on page 104.*

Applying shellac stick with a burn-in knife
You can buy special burn-in kits for applying shellac sticks. The typical package includes a burn-in knife with a gently bent, stainless steel blade; an alcohol lamp for heating the knife; and a special solution for soaking a felt block that levels the repair with the surrounding surface. Light the alcohol torch and hold the burn-in knife over the wick for several seconds. Press the knife against the stick so that enough filler melts and drips into the hole *(left)*. Make sure that the shellac does not bubble when it contacts the knife or the product will damage the surrounding finish. Reheat the knife as necessary until the hole is filled. Use the knife to spread the filler evenly, then level the repair as shown below.

LEVELING MELTED SHELLAC

Using a felt block and leveling solution
Whether you have used a soldering gun or a burn-in knife to melt shellac into a gouge, you need to level the filler with the surrounding surface. Soak the bottom of a felt block with a small amount of commercial leveling solution and lightly rub the block back and forth across the repair *(right)*. The slow-acting solvent in the solution dissolves excess filler without harming the wood or the finish. Once the filler has been leveled, refinish the affected area *(page 100)*.

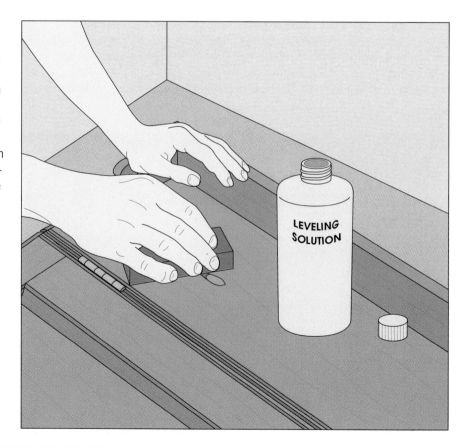

REPAIRING DENTS

Lifting a dent with steam

One way to fix a dent in wood is to swell crushed fibers to their original shape. (Note: Since you are relying on heat and moisture to effect this repair, you cannot use the technique on finishes that are damaged by heat or moisture, such as shellac.) Turn a household iron to its highest setting and allow it to heat up. Meanwhile, dampen a clean cloth with water, fold it into a pad, and place it on the dent. Press the tip of the iron against the cloth over the dent *(right)*, holding it in place until the cloth steams. The steam will swell the wood fibers, lifting out the dent. Add water to the cloth as necessary and avoid leaving the iron on the cloth for too long, as this may scorch the wood. If the steam does not work, or the finish is shellac, try filling the dent *(step below)*.

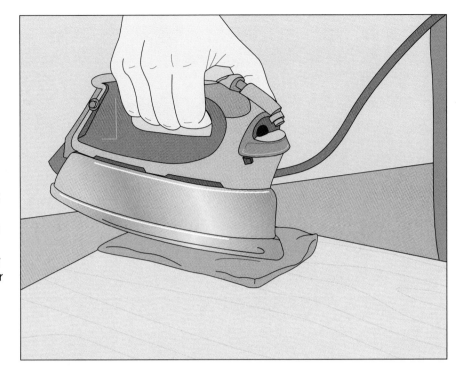

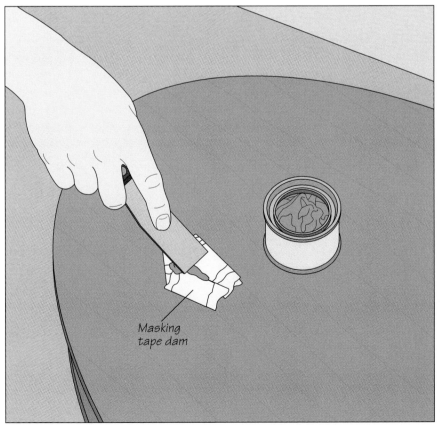

Masking
tape dam

Filling the dent

Apply a few layers of masking tape on each side of the dent, forming a dam. Since most wood fillers shrink as they dry, the dam will enable you to overfill the cavity and eliminate the need for a second application. It will also protect the surrounding finish from the filler. Choose a filler that is compatible with the ingredients and color of the finish you will be applying. Use a putty knife to work the filler into the hole and overfill it slightly, then scrape off the excess to level it with the masking tape *(left)*. Once the filler is dry, carefully remove the tape and sand the area flush with surrounding finish. You can now refinish the area *(page 100)*.

FILLING EDGES, CORNERS AND CONTOURED SURFACES

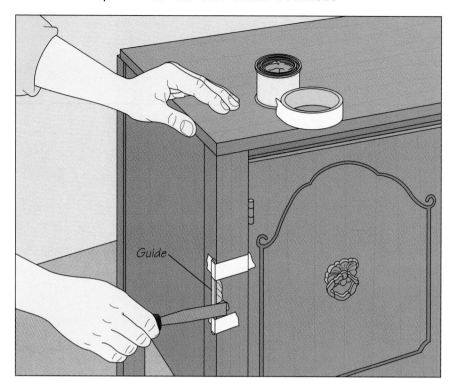

Guide

Repairing a broken edge
You can use wood filler to reconstruct a damaged edge. Align a thin piece of metal or plastic, or a tongue depressor against the adjacent edge and tape it in place to serve as a guide. Apply the filler with a putty knife *(left)*, using the same procedure as for filling a dent *(page 105)*.

SHOP TIP

Concentrating the steam to lift a dent
The technique for raising a dent with steam shown on page 105 is ideal for larger blemishes, but for small dents, it is better to focus the steam to a confined area. Use a soldering gun and a bottle cap, as shown at right. Heat up the gun and place a dampened cloth over the dent. Then position a bottle cap, corrugated-side down, on the cloth directly over the blemish. Touch the tip of the gun to the cap until the cloth steams. As with the household iron, the steam will swell the wood fibers and lift up the dent.

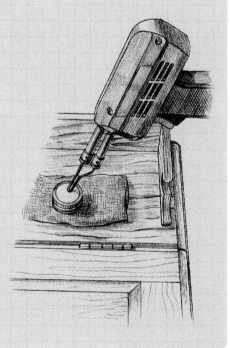

Repairing a broken corner

Make a form to keep the filler from sagging by taping pieces of metal or plastic, or tongue depressors on both sides of the corner. The top edges of the form should be flush with the top of the workpiece and the angle formed by the sticks should be exactly 90°. Press wood filler into the cavity using a putty knife *(right)*, overfilling it slightly. Scrape the excess to level the filler with the surrounding surface, then refinish the repair *(page 100)*.

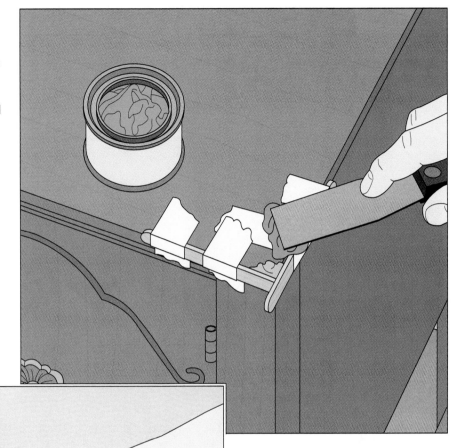

Repairing a contoured surface

To patch an irregular surface, such as the turned leg shown at left, you can use wood-filling epoxy. When mixed, this product is firm enough to form into the required shape, and it dries quickly. Prepare the epoxy following the manufacturer's directions; typically, two parts—a resin and a hardener—must be mixed together. Use a putty knife to apply the filler to the damaged area, trying to sculpt it to the required shape. Let the filler harden, then finish shaping it with a rasp or a file. Refinish the area *(page 100)*.

Wood-filling epoxy

REFINISHING

When the finish on an antique is beyond repair, or is unsuited to the style and age of the piece, it is time to strip it and apply a new one. Although the process can be messy, few restoration projects can so dramatically transform a piece of furniture's appearance. Stripping can yield pleasant surprises: Imagine the satisfaction of lifting off several layers of paint from a tabletop and discovering the mellow, pink hue of plain-sawn cherry. But not every refinishing job is such a thorough and transfiguring venture; sometimes, brushing a solvent onto a damaged finish and rubbing it down with steel wool will do the trick nicely.

Refinishing is a field rife with conflicting opinions. As a result, there are no hard and fast rules about what methods and products are ideal in every situation. However, there is greater agreement on the appropriate solvents and tools for various finishes. The chart on page 110 lists a number of commonly used chemical strippers along with their characteristics and the precautions to be taken when using them. Various techniques for stripping finishes are described beginning on page 111, from using steel wool and burlap to scraping with a putty knife or a toothbrush.

Before applying a new finish, you may need to prepare the wood surface by smoothing it with a hand scraper *(page*

The antique stool shown above is being finished with milk paint, a traditional furniture finish. Milk paint is available in powder form and mixed with water to a paint-like consistency. Like any paint, this finish is best applied with a good-quality brush.

116), brushing on a pore filler *(page 120)* to achieve a glossy sheen, or staining the wood to the desired color *(page 121).* The chapter also explores many common finishing products and techniques, from antique recipes *(page 121)* to French polishing *(page 132).* Specialty finishes *(page 138)* are also discussed.

Before starting a refinishing project, keep the following rules in mind. Place the workpiece on a tarp or plastic sheet, and cover nearby surfaces. Also protect upholstery, glass, and the insides of drawers with newspaper and masking tape. Remove hardware from the piece and make any necessary repairs, such as regluing loose veneer. Work outdoors or in a well-ventilated area indoors.

There are times when you may wish to seek out a professional restorer to do the work. Choose one carefully; obtain references from other woodworkers who have had work done by restorers, or ask local antique dealers. Before entrusting an antique to a professional, visit the premises and check out the shop's level of tidiness, safety and, if possible, the quality of any work on hand. Find out whether dip tanks are used for stripping. If so, you may want to look elsewhere; dip tanks remove finishes aggressively and can be damaging to the wood.

The clock door at left is being refinished with a traditional French polish. Before applying the finish, the surface was cleaned with alcohol and 4/0 steel wool. To develop the deep, glossy sheen of a French polish, pumice is sprinkled on the surface and several coats of shellac are rubbed on with a wool-and-linen pad moistened with alcohol.

STRIPPING FINISHES

Too often, inexperienced furniture strippers forget that the chemicals should do most of the work, and instead try to hurry the job with aggressive scraping and rubbing. The results can be damaging to the furniture. Experienced hands let the solvent do the work, using just enough mechanical action to clean the wood surface. With the wide range of stripping agents available, choosing the right method for the job at hand can appear baffling. But remember that most commercial products are essentially the same, with methylene chloride as the main component—present in most popular brands of stripper at concentrations of about 80 percent. This and some other commonly used stripper solutions are listed in the chart below. Before choosing a stripping agent, try to identify the finish *(page 96)* so you can select the least aggressive stripper for the job. For example, denatured alcohol will remove shellac *(page 111)* and lacquer thinner will soften lacquer. For varnish or an enamel finish *(page 112)*, you will have to resort to a stronger formulation, such as methylene chloride.

Safety is a prime consideration when stripping finishes. Despite claims made by some manufacturers, chemical strippers are generally hazardous; some solvents are thought to be cancer-causing if their fumes are ingested in large quantities. Work outdoors, weather permitting. If you must strip indoors, make sure the area is well ventilated and protect nearby surfaces with dropcloths or corrosion-resistant vinyl. In either case, protect yourself with the appropriate safety gear. Wear safety goggles, a dual-cartridge respirator, a long-sleeved shirt with the sleeves rolled down, and corrosion-resistant gloves. To provide added protection for your hands and facilitate cleaning them afterwards, apply a layer of skin cleanser before donning the gloves.

An ammonia-based solvent is being brushed onto a painted chair. Within a few minutes, the solvent will soften the finish so it can be scrubbed off with 2/0 steel wool. Any residual paint can be removed with a scraper. Because ammonia can darken wood, applying an oxalic acid solution after stripping will restore the original color.

COMMON STRIPPING AGENTS

SOLVENTS	CHARACTERISTICS	SAFETY PRECAUTIONS
Methylene chloride, methanol (MC)	Will remove almost any finish	Produces toxic fumes; work outdoors or in a well-ventilated area indoors
Acetone, toluene and chloride (ATM)	Less expensive than MC solvents, but almost as effective	Flammable and produces toxic fumes; work outdoors or in a well-ventilated area indoors
N-methyl pyrrolidone (NMP)	Takes up to three times as long to work as the MC solvent and more expensive	Safer than MC solvents due to slower evaporation rate
Di-basic ester (DBE)	Requires standing time of up to 12 hours; less effective on shellac and lacquer	Safer than MC solvents
MC/ATM (solvent combination)	Will remove most finishes; less expensive than straight, MC solvents	Flammable and produces toxic fumes; work outdoors or in a well-ventilated area indoors
NMP/DBE (solvent comination)	Faster than DBE solvents; more expensive and less effective than MC solvents	Safer than MC solvents due to slower evaporation rate
Methylene chloride /methanol/ ammonium hydroxide (solvent combination)	The strongest and fastest acting of all strippers; use when others are ineffective. Can stain some hardwoods	Produces toxic fumes; work outdoors or in a well-ventilated area indoors

TREATING A SHELLAC FINISH

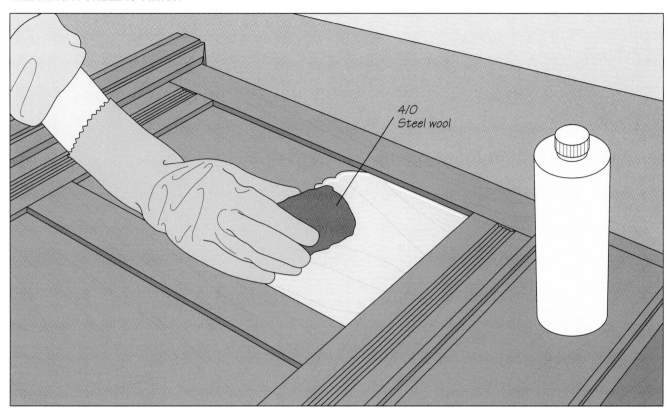

4/0
Steel wool

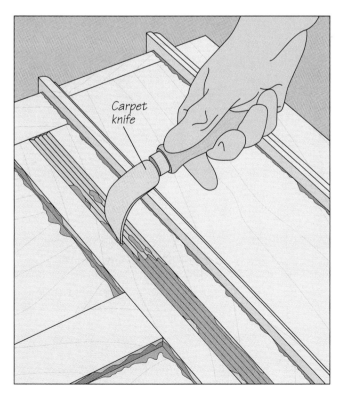

Carpet
knife

1 Stripping flat surfaces

If a shellac finish is stained or contains embedded dirt, but is still basically sound, you may not have to strip it. Instead, sprinkle a mild abrasive compound, such as pumice or rotten-stone, on the surface; work it in and rub it off with a cloth. This should remove most of the dirt and staining. Avoid using a lubricant as this could damage the finish and may not be necessary if the stain is not too serious. Buff the surface lightly with a clean rag to give it some shine. If the stain is deeper, you will have to strip the finish. Use denatured alcohol and 4/0 steel wool. Brush the alcohol on the surface and let it soak into the finish for several minutes, or until it dissolves the finish. Wearing rubber gloves, rub off as much of the finish-and-stripper mixture as you can with the steel wool (above), then remove the rest with a rag.

2 Stripping curved surfaces and recesses

Use a carpet knife to remove the finish-and-stripper mixture from surfaces you cannot reach with the steel wool. For the crevices of a fluted surface, as shown at left, place the pointed tip of the knife and scrape the sludge out of the furrows (left). Clean off the mixture with a rag.

REMOVING AN ENAMEL FINISH

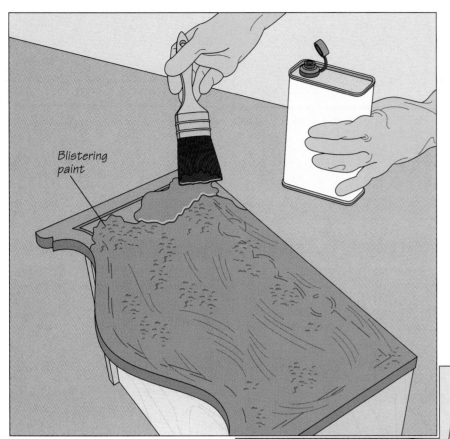

Blistering paint

1 Applying the stripper
Paint and enamel finishes are best removed with one of the commercial stripping agents listed on page 110. Wearing corrosion-resistant gloves, safety goggles, and a dual-cartridge respirator, pour a liberal amount of the stripper onto all the flat horizontal surfaces of the workpiece, then use a wide paintbrush to spread the solution into a thick, even coat *(left)*. For vertical and contoured surfaces, use the brush to apply the stripper as thick as possible without dripping. Let the stripper stand on the surface for the time specified by the manufacturer, usually several minutes. Once the finish begins to blister, let the solution stand for about 10 more minutes. You will then be ready to remove the finish-and-stripper mixture *(step 2)*.

2 Scraping the stripper and finish from flat surfaces
Use a wide, flat-bladed paint scraper or putty knife to remove the finish-and-stripper from the flat surfaces of the workpiece. Holding the blade at an angle to the surface, push it along the surface, lifting the softened mixture from the wood *(right)*. To remove stubborn residue or clean out crevices, try using a stiff toothbrush or a brass-bristled brush, as shown on page 114. Brass is softer that steel, and broken bristles do not rust and stain.

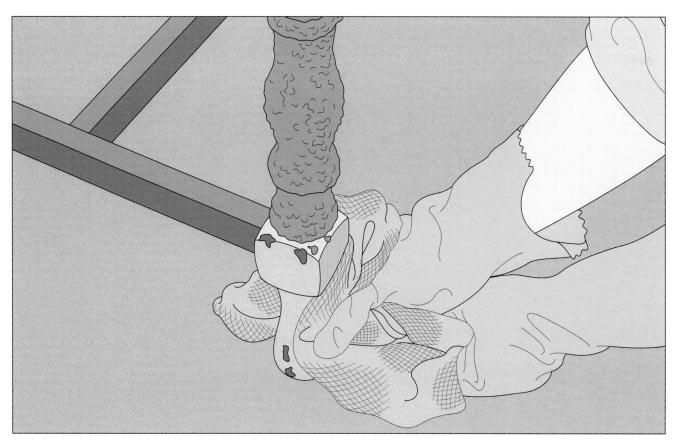

3 Removing the finish and stripper from contoured surface

For turned or molded surfaces that are awkward to scrape clean with a putty knife or scraper, such as the table leg shown above, use a piece of burlap. Holding the burlap in one hand, grasp the surface and rub it up-and-down and side-to-side to clean off the residue.

SHOP TIP

Using sawdust as a wiping aid
The coarse sawdust produced by a planer is ideal for removing a finish-and-stripper mixture from a piece of furniture. Apply the stripper as described on page 112 and simply sprinkle some sawdust on the surface. Then wipe off all the residue with a rag. Alternatively, you can hold some of the sawdust in your gloved hand and use it to scrape off the residue.

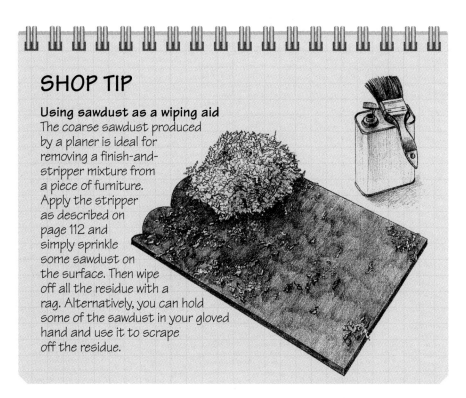

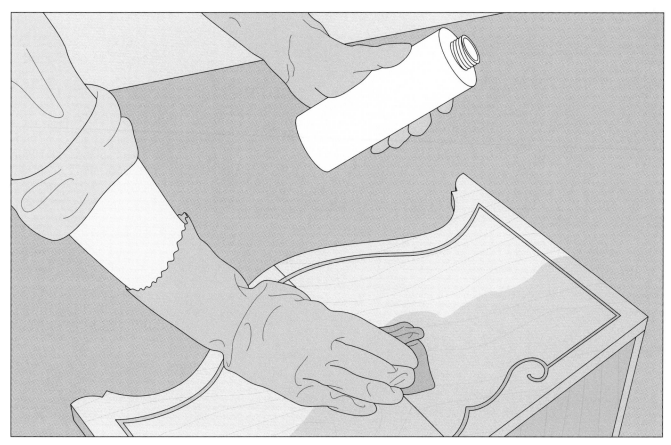

4 **Neutralizing the surface**
After using a stripper, it is important to neutralize the chemical residue left on the surface of the workpiece. This will ensure that no lasting harm will be done to the wood, and that the finish you apply later will adhere properly to the surface. For most strippers, use trisodium phosphate or a borax-based soap. Moisten a clean rag with the neutralizing agent and wipe the stripped surface thoroughly *(above)*.

SHOP TIP

Removing stripper residue from a carving
To scrape a stripper-and-finish mixture from a carved surface or any crevice in the surface, use a toothbrush or a brass-bristled brush. Apply the stripper and let it blister *(page 112)*, then work the bristles into any tight spots to remove the residue.

STRIPPING PAINT WITH A HEAT GUN

1 Heating the finish
A heat gun is an effective alternative to chemical strippers for removing paint finishes from furniture. The heat will cause the paint to blister and separate from the wood surface. Following the manufacturer's instructions, turn on the gun and let it warm up to its maximum temperature. Holding the nozzle a few inches from the finish at one end of the surface, pass the gun over the paint until it begins to blister and lift from the wood *(left)*. Once the paint blisters, scrape it off *(step 2)* and move on to the next section. Avoid holding the gun steady over one section of the surface for longer than necessary; this could damage the wood.

2 Scraping the paint from the surface
Holding a putty knife or a flat-bladed paint scraper in your free hand, scrape the softened paint off the surface *(right)*. Use the technique described on page 112 for removing stripper-and-finish residues. Continue heating the finish and scraping it off, section by section, until you have removed all of the paint.

PREPARING SURFACES FOR A FINISH

A sanding stick smooths the back rail of a chair. This device is ideal for reaching into tight spots, such as the spaces between the slats of a backrest.

Once the old finish has been stripped from a piece of furniture, you can often apply a new finish without any further preparation. In fact, in many cases, you are better off skipping over the surface treatments presented in this section of the chapter. It all depends on the condition and appearance of the piece, and on the effect you are attempting to achieve.

Many antiques, for example, derive part of their character from the mellowed patina of the surface—even from minor blemishes such as scratches and gouges. If you take a hand scraper or sanding block to this sort of piece of furniture, you will no doubt smooth and even out the surface, but you also risk destroying some of the charm of the piece, diminishing both its value and appearance.

In other cases, a piece may need some preparation before you can apply a finish. The surface may be too rough or uneven, or it may have unsightly dents and knicks. One of the best tools for smoothing such surfaces is a hand scraper *(below)*. Although scrapers take practice to use, they impart a very smooth finish, and can reduce your sanding time once you master the technique. Sanding with successively finer grits *(page 117)* completes the surface preparation.

Whether or not to fill the pores of the wood *(page 120)* is a matter of taste. If you are planning to apply a natural-looking finish that does not obscure the wood grain, do not use filler. Close-grained species such as pine or cherry should never be filled, but if you want a glossy finish on an open-grained wood, such as oak or mahogany, you must fill it.

SCRAPING

Using a hand scraper
A hand scraper can remove high spots, tearout, and other flaws from the surface of a workpiece. Standing at one end of the surface, curl your fingers around the front of the scraper and press on the back with your thumbs to make the tool bow slightly outward. Tilt the scraper forward about 20° from the vertical and scrape the surface in the direction that the bow is facing *(right)*. The scraper should remove paper-thin wood shavings. If the cutting edge does not bite into the wood properly, adjust the angle of the tool slightly. Work at a slight angle to the grain, applying moderate pressure and making long, fluid, overlapping strokes. At the end of each stroke, lift the scraper off the surface before stopping. You can also pull the scraper, but be sure to flex the bow toward you.

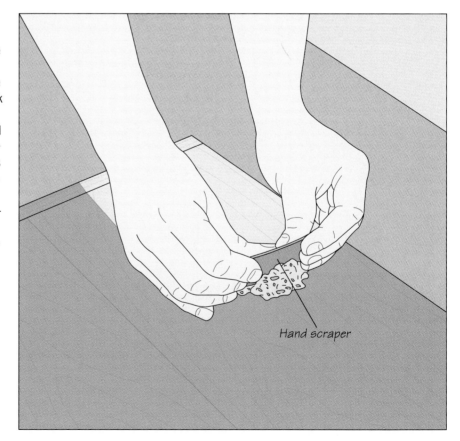

Hand scraper

SANDING FLAT SURFACES

Hand sanding

To remove scratches from a flat surface, use a sanding block. Attach a piece of sandpaper of the appropriate grit to the block. Then gripping the device firmly, sand the surface with straight, overlapping, back-and-forth strokes, applying moderate pressure and working with the grain of the wood *(left)*. Keep the block flat on the surface at all times, particularly when you reach an end or edge.

SANDING CONTOURED SURFACES

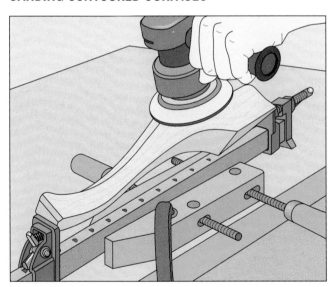

Using a power sander

With its compact and pliable sanding pad, the random-orbit sander is ideal for smoothing contours such as a cabriole leg *(above)*. (In this example, the leg has been detached from the furniture.) Secure the workpiece in a bar clamp, grip the clamp in a handscrew, and clamp the handscrew to a work surface. Fasten a sanding disk to the sander's pad. With the tool clear of the stock, switch it on and lower the pad onto the surface. Applying moderate pressure, work along the length of the workpiece in back-and-forth passes until the surface is smooth. Work carefully—power sanders remove stock quickly. Reposition the piece in the clamp as necessary to smooth adjacent surfaces.

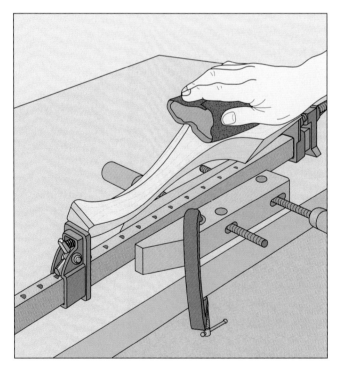

Hand sanding

Smoothing contoured surfaces using only a power sander risks creating blemishes on the wood or flattening out the curves with excessive pressure. For a shop-made sanding pad that can follow contours without oversanding, wrap a sheet of sandpaper around a thick sponge that you can grip comfortably. Then sand along the length of the surface, pressing firmly on the stock *(above)*.

ABRASIVE GRADES AND GRITS

SANDPAPER		
Grade	**Grit**	**Uses**
Medium	80, 100, 120	Initial smoothing; removing shallow depressions and scratches
Fine	150, 180	Intermediate smoothing
Very fine	220, 240	Final smoothing before applying a finish
Extra fine	280, 320 360, 400	Removing dust particles and air bubbles between finish coats Final sanding before final coat of finish; initial sanding for high-gloss finish
Super fine	600, 1200	Rubbing down the final coat of high-gloss finish
STEEL WOOL		
Grade	**Grit**	**Uses**
Medium	1	Light removal of particles and raised fibers; smoothing of shallow depressions and scratches
Fine	00	Smoothing before applying a clear finish
Extra fine	000	Smoothing between coats of finish; light cleaning and deglossing of a finish or polish
Super fine	0000	Polishing; waxing

Choosing sandpaper
The range of sandpaper in the chart above will serve for almost any finishing job. When buying sandpaper, consider its composition. Aluminum oxide is the most efficient and long-lasting for the price. Choose papers with grits above 220 for sanding when restoring a finish.

SHOP TIP

Making a sandpaper cutting board
To cut sheets of sandpaper quickly and accurately, use a shop-made cutting board. Screw a hacksaw blade to a piece of plywood with a washer under each end to raise it slightly off the plywood. To cut a sandpaper sheet in half, slide it under the blade. Holding one end down, tear the other part of the sheet off. Tear a sheet in half, and then tear each half in half again for four equal quarters.

RAISING THE GRAIN

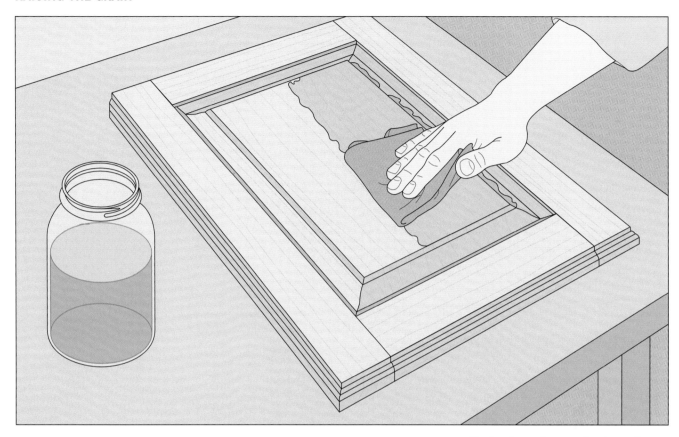

SHOP TIP

Making a tack cloth
Make a tack cloth to match the finishing product you intend to use. For a water-based finish, simply dampen a clean piece of cheesecloth with water. For a solvent-based finish, dampen the cloth with mineral spirits, then work in a few drops of varnish. Squeeze the cloth repeatedly until it begins to feel sticky. Add varnish when it loses its tacky feel. Store a tack cloth in a plastic bag with a label identifying it as either water- or solvent-based.

Wetting the surface to raise the grain
Every phase of working with wood—from jointing and sawing the boards to planing and scraping them—compresses the fibers on the surface. Exposure to water causes the fibers to stand up, roughening the surface. If you intend to use a water-based finish, wet the surface to raise the grain before applying the finishing solution. Wet a rag with water and squeeze it out to leave it damp, rub the surface lightly, then wipe off the excess with a clean cloth *(above)*. Allow the surface to dry, then lightly scuff the wood with a very fine (220-grit) sandpaper. Avoid oversanding, which might expose the fresh grain, making it necessary to repeat the process and destroy the patina of the wood.

FILLING THE GRAIN

1 Brushing on the filler

Filling the wood grain is the most effective way to achieve a high-gloss, mirror-like finish on open-grained woods such as ash or oak. Pour some of the grain filler, also known as pore filler or paste wood filler, into a container. Apply the filler with a paintbrush *(above)*; you can also use abrasive pads. Using back-and-forth, overlapping strokes, cover the surface completely, working with the grain. Examine the workpiece—in this case, a frame-and-panel door—under direct light to confirm that the surface is covered thoroughly. Apply more filler, if necessary.

2 Wiping off excess filler

Once the filler begins to dry, loses its shine and turns hazy, wipe it with a piece of clean burlap folded into a pad *(right)*. Starting at one end of the workpiece, work with a circular motion to pack the filler into the pores of the wood and wipe the panel first, then remove the excess. On a detailed workpiece such as a raised panel, wipe the panel first, then remove excess filler from hard-to-reach spots with a sharpened dowel wrapped in a clean piece of burlap. Allow the filler to dry, then smooth the surface with 220- to 320-grit sandpaper. If a second coat is required, apply it the same way.

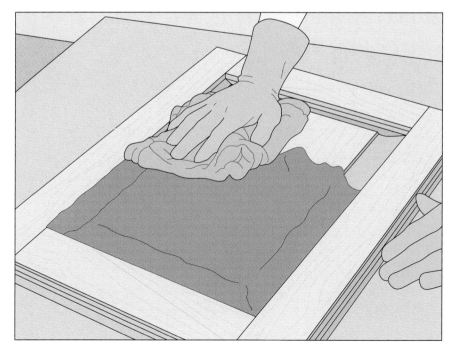

STAINING THE WOOD

Stains are as old as furniture making itself. They have helped common woods take on the appearance of more desirable species, adding color and emphasizing figure. They have also been used to create a uniform appearance when different woods are used in the same workpiece.

Modern stains fall into two broad categories: those with dyes and those containing pigments. Dyes impart translucent color to wood, altering nature's palette while leaving the intricate grain patterns visible. Pigment stains contain opaque colorants that cling to the surface of the wood. The chart on page 123 lists several examples of both types, describing solvents to use, the characteristics of the stains and how to prepare and apply them.

In furniture restoration, staining may be necessary to blend a repair into the surrounding wood or to alter the color and character of an antique. The charts below list stains that you can buy premixed or create yourself by combining the appropriate ingredients. As described at left, some experimentation is usually necessary before you hit on the perfect formulation.

A powdered aniline dye is added to a glass container for mixing with the appropriate solvent to produce a stain. You can take the guesswork out of staining by applying a sample to an inconspicuous surface of the workpiece and letting it dry. Then adjust the color, if necessary, by adding powder to darken it or more solvent to lighten it.

CHOOSING A STAIN

For some staining jobs, a premixed stain may be all that you need. The chart below *(left)* lists some popular commercial formulations. To replicate the color of a particular antique, however, it may be necessary to create a stain by mixing dyes or pigments with the appropriate solvent. The chart below, at right, describes recipes commonly used on antique furniture.

PREMIXED STAINS
• Mahogany: A reddish hue, sometimes verging on brown
• Light Oak: Commonly sandy or tan-colored
• Walnut: Brown
• Maple: Orange, leaning toward yellow
• Black: Usually used to dampen livelier colors

COMMON STAIN RECIPES	
COLOR DESIRED	**DYES OR PIGMENTS**
Antique Pine	4 parts Walnut, 1 part Mahogany
Brown Mahogany	5 parts Walnut, 1 part Mahogany, 1 part Oak
Antique Maple	2 parts Maple, 1 part Oak, 1 part Walnut
Honey Maple	3 parts Oak, 2 parts Maple, 1 part Walnut,
Cherry	1 part Walnut, 1 part Oak, 1 part Mahogany
Fruitwood	4 parts Oak, 1 part Maple, 1 part Walnut
Dark Oak	1 part Walnut, 1 part Oak
Swedish Walnut	4 parts Walnut, 2 parts Oak, one drop of black
Red Cherry	1 part Mahogany, 1 part Walnut

APPLYING A STAIN

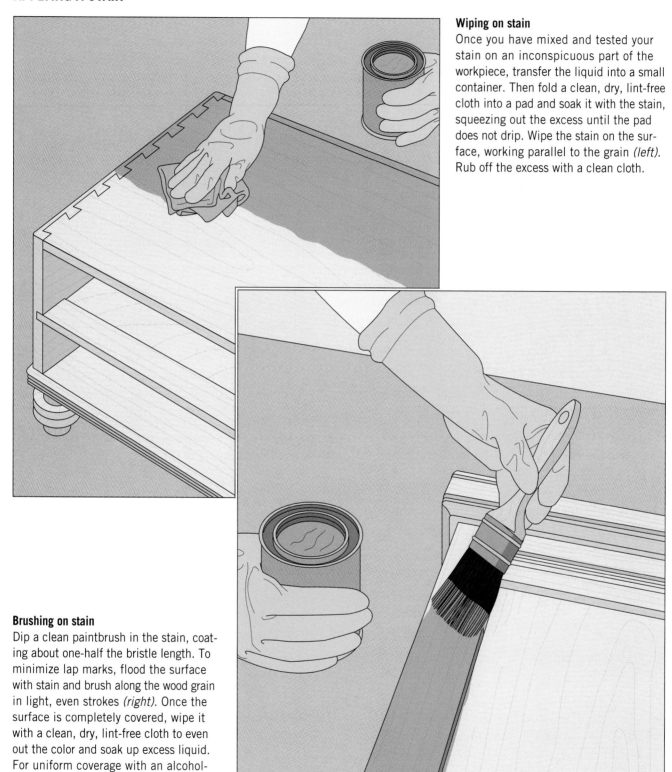

Wiping on stain
Once you have mixed and tested your stain on an inconspicuous part of the workpiece, transfer the liquid into a small container. Then fold a clean, dry, lint-free cloth into a pad and soak it with the stain, squeezing out the excess until the pad does not drip. Wipe the stain on the surface, working parallel to the grain *(left)*. Rub off the excess with a clean cloth.

Brushing on stain
Dip a clean paintbrush in the stain, coating about one-half the bristle length. To minimize lap marks, flood the surface with stain and brush along the wood grain in light, even strokes *(right)*. Once the surface is completely covered, wipe it with a clean, dry, lint-free cloth to even out the color and soak up excess liquid. For uniform coverage with an alcohol-based stain, wipe the surface as soon as possible after brushing it on.

GALLERY OF STAINS

DYE STAINS

TYPE	AVAILABLE FORM	CHARACTERISTICS AND USES	PREPARATION AND APPLICATION
Water-based stain	Powdered; water-soluble	Penetrating; not very lightfast; transparent; brilliant; tends to raise grain; good for hardwoods; compatible with any finish	Raise grain *(page 119)*. Add to water and strain. Apply with brush, rag, or spray gun.
Spirit stain	Powdered; alcohol-soluble	Penetrating; not lightfast; dries quickly, but tends to leave lap and streak marks	Mix with alcohol and strain. Brush or wipe on. Best for small areas.
Oil stain	Powdered; oil-soluble	Penetrating; transparent; does not obscure grain; slow-drying; bleeds; needs sealer coat of shellac; good for softwoods	Dissolve in mineral spirits or petroleum distillate and strain. Apply with nylon-bristle brush and wipe off excess.
NGR stain	Liquid; dissolved in methanol and petroleum distillate solution	Does not raise grain; transparent and lightfast; good for veneers	Thin to desired consistency. Apply with spray gun. If applying with a brush or rag, use retarder.
Penetrating oil stain	Liquid; dissolved in mineral spirits	Penetrates open-grained wood; moderately lightfast; transparent; easy to apply; colors can be mixed; does not raise or obscure grain; bleeds; needs wash coat; good choice for softwoods	Apply with brush or rag. Wipe off excess after desired color is achieved.
Varnish stain	Liquid; dissolved in varnish	Highly transparent; lightfast; non-penetrating; adds filler, color, and gloss in one operation; good for lower grades of lumber	Apply with a rag and wipe off, or use a spray gun.

PIGMENT STAINS

TYPE	AVAILABLE FORM	CHARACTERISTICS AND USES	PREPARATION AND APPLICATION
Wiping stain	Liquid; suspended in oil and mineral spirits	Lightfast; will not bleed; non-penetrating; opaque; tends to hide grain	Apply with brush, rag, or spray gun. Wipe off excess after desired color is achieved.
Earth pigment	Powder; soluble in any liquid	Easy to use; lightfast; opaque; hides grain; good for wood with indistinct grain or for tinting protective finish	Mix with oil or varnish. Apply with brush, rag, or spray gun.
Japan color	Liquid; concentrated in varnish	Excellent for tinting varnish, stain, lacquer	Apply with synthetic brush.
Gel stain	Liquid; suspended in petroleum-based gel	Easy to use; hides grain	Apply with rag; wipe off excess after desired color is achieved.
Glazing stain	Liquid; suspended in varnish	Excellent for figuring, shading, or correcting sap streaks; hides grain; wears off; needs a hard-finish coat	Apply with brush or rag; allow to set. Wipe off with grain if desired.
Water-based stain	Liquid; suspended in an acrylic and water base	Non-penetrating; lightfast; brilliant; colors can be mixed together; nontoxic and nonflammable	Raise grain *(page 119)*. Apply with brush, rag, or spray gun.

Staining a carved surface
To work stain into all the folds and crevices of a carved surface, use a small artist's brush. Dip the bristles in the stain and carefully brush it onto any areas that you could not reach with a rag or a larger brush *(above)*.

SHOP TIP

Preparing a natural walnut stain
To make "brou de noix," a natural walnut dye stain popular in the 1800's, collect enough green walnut husks to fill half a large, nonstick steel pot. Let the husks dry and turn black, then soak them in the pot with enough water to cover them completely. Add one tablespoon of lye for every gallon of the mixture. Then simmer the mixture over low heat for several days, adding water periodically. Bottle the solution in clear glass jars and leave them in bright sunlight until the mixture darkens further. Strain the dye through an old cloth and rebottle it, discarding the husks. Applied with a brush, "brou de noix" produces a range of rich brown tones on wood.

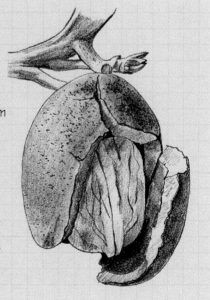

BLEACHING WOOD

Bleaches are highly reactive chemicals that break down the natural colorants in wood and woodworkers have used them for centuries to lighten the color of their stock. The effect can be startling. Walnut, a wood known for its deep, brown color turns a creamy shade of grey when it is bleached, as shown in the photo at right.

For the furniture restorer, bleaching can be a useful technique to match two different woods by bleaching the darker species to simulate the lighter one. It can also be effective in removing an old aniline dye or a stubborn stain from a workpiece. Other stain-removal techniques are explained starting on page 98.

There are three common types of wood bleach. Oxalic acid, sold in liquid form as "deck brightener," is your best choice for eliminating stains from wood.

Sodium hypochlorite will do an excellent job of removing an aniline dye from a workpiece. This product is available as liquid laundry bleach. But the most effective all-purpose wood lightener is two part A/B wood bleach. Using this variety of bleach involves combining lye and peroxide; the resulting effect is stronger than that of either ingredient on its own.

Exercise caution when using bleach. It can corrode tools and harm skin. Wear rubber gloves and use a synthetic brush or sponge to apply bleach; a natural-bristle brush will eventually disintegrate in the solution. Mix and store bleach in glass containers; the chemicals may react with metal. Never mix bleach with another chemical, and always follow manufacturer's instructions for proper handling and use.

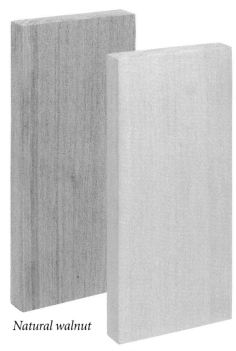

Natural walnut

Bleached walnut

APPLYING THE BLEACH

Applying bleach

Remove dirt and oil from the surface, then prepare the solution. For two-part A/B bleach, pour a quantity of each into separate glass bowls. Do not mix the two parts together; they will be applied in separate steps. Spread a generous but even coat of Part A on the wood surface with a paint brush or sponge *(left)*. Let the product do its work for about 5 minutes, then apply Part B the same way. Let the workpiece sit for at least 4 hours, then rinse the surface with water or the neutralizer supplied with the bleach. Allow the workpiece to dry overnight before applying a stain or a finish. Two-part bleach is usually strong enough so that one application will be sufficient; however you can repeat the process to lighten the wood further.

APPLYING A PROTECTIVE FINISH

Once you have stripped the old finish off an antique, prepared the surface and, perhaps, stained or bleached it, it is time to apply a protective finish that will enhance and preserve the wood's appearance. This section explores the characteristics and application methods for five surface treatments commonly used on furniture: drying oils, such as tung and walnut oil, varnish, polyurethane, shellac, and lacquer.

There are no hard and fast rules governing which finish is best for a particular piece of furniture. Of course, if your goal is to restore the piece to its original condition, then ideally you should apply the same type of finish that you stripped off. On a piece built before the advent of modern synthetic finishes like varnish and polyurethane, your options are usually narrowed down to the finishes most commonly found on antiques—shellac, lacquer, or a drying oil.

Finishes not only contribute to the authenticity and appearance of a piece; they also protect the wood from the environment to which it is exposed. As a result, you should also consider the function your piece will serve once you have restored it. If the piece is likely to be exposed to moisture or heat, then a finish like shellac may be a poor choice, since it resists neither water nor heat. Varnish and polyurethane dry to a hard and tough film, making them good choices for pieces that will be subject to abuse. On the other hand, shellac lends itself well to spot-repairs, whereas a damaged varnish or polyurethane finish must usually be stripped off and redone.

Denatured alcohol is being added to shellac resin to form a spreadable finish. Once mixed, the solution can be brushed onto a workpiece. Shellac is classified according to its "pound cut," which refers to the amount of resin dissolved in the solvent. A 1-pound-cut shellac, for example, has one pound of resin for each gallon of solvent. A 5-pound cut contains 5 pounds of shellac for every gallon of solvent.

DRYING OILS

Drying oils, such as tung and walnut oil, are a group of natural finishes that cure to form a relatively hard film on a wood surface. These clear finishes are flooded onto the wood and the excess is wiped, leaving a thin film to dry. One or two coats seal the surface and subsequent layers can be applied to add thickness or sheen. Even today, the term "hand-rubbed finish" conjures up an image of luster and quality. Tung oil, also known as China wood oil, is one of the most popular drying oil finishes. Extracted from the nut of the tung tree, the oil is available in pure, modified and polymerized form.

The main benefit of modified tung oil is that it contains chemical additives that allow it to dry more quickly. Polymerized tung oil undergoes a special heat treatment; it dries faster still and produces a glossier surface.

Drying oils are reactive finishes, meaning that they dry and harden when exposed to air—even in a sealed container. When you store a drying oil, use a container that is as small as possible to reduce the volume of air to which the oil is exposed.

APPLICATION SEQUENCE

1. Wipe the oil onto the surface with a cloth; it should be applied straight from the container.
2. Let the oil soak into the wood (typically for 15 minutes), then use a clean cloth to wipe off the excess.
3. Let the surface dry, usually overnight.
4. Sand the surface with 400-grit paper and remove sanding particles.
5. Repeat steps 1 to 4 as many times as necessary to achieve the finish you want. Depending on the wood, five coats of oil will typically yield a semigloss sheen.
6. Let the surface cure for at least a week before rubbing out the finish *(page 130)*.

VARNISH

Varnish is a highly durable protective coat for wood, more resistant to heat and alcohol damage than products like shellac and lacquer. It is also relatively easy to apply. While you are brushing it on, try to work with a white wall or a window in back of the workpiece. The backlighting will help you see if you are skipping an area or picking up any dust.

Varnishes were once made with natural resins and oils like linseed oil. These materials have since been supplanted by synthetic resins, but the old system of classifying varnish based on the proportion of oil-to-resin still prevails.

Accordingly, varnishes are designated as either short, medium, or long oil. Long-oil varnish is slow-drying, producing a soft and elastic coating. Short-oil varnish is hard, and glossy. Medium-oil varnish provides a finish that falls between the two in terms of gloss and durability.

APPLICATION SEQUENCE

1. Dilute the varnish according to the manufacturer's directions and spread a thin coat on the surface with a high-quality bristle brush or a foam brush; work first against the grain, then with it.

2. Let the surface dry, typically for 12 to 24 hours.

3. Sand the surface with a self-lubricating 240- or 280-grit sandpaper.

4. Repeat steps 1 to 3, using a stronger dilution of varnish and sanding the surface with a finer-grit sandpaper (280- to 320-grit).

5. Brush on an undiluted coat of varnish.

6. Let the surface dry and sand with 400-grit sandpaper.

7. Repeat steps 5 and 6 two or three times.

8. Let the surface cure for 24 to 72 hours before rubbing out the finish (page 130).

POLYURETHANE

Polyurethane is a transparent, varnish-like finish that is durable, abrasion-resistant and easy to apply. Formulated with synthetic resin, it dries more quickly than varnish, making it an ideal choice when you have limited time for finishing work.

Polyurethanes are available in a variety of lusters, ranging from flat to glossy. Because they do not release toxic solvents into the atmosphere while drying, water-based polyurethanes are safer for the environment than their solvent-based counterparts.

APPLICATION SEQUENCE

1. Apply a thin and even coat with a paintbrush or pad applicator, always brushing with the grain.

2. Let the surface dry for about 2 hours.

3. Sand the surface with a 320- to 400-grit sandpaper.

4. Repeat steps 1 to 3, with a finer-grit sandpaper.

5. Apply a final coat, giving the surface 18 to 24 hours to dry before rubbing out the finish (page 130).

SHELLAC

Shellac is a natural finish produced from the secretions of the lac insect, which is indigenous to Indochina and India. The bugs feed on tree sap and expel a resin that forms a protective shell around their bodies. Eventually this material builds up and is deposited on tree twigs and branches; it is then harvested and processed.

In its commercial forms, shellac is available both in a liquid and in flakes. Liquid shellac is ready for use, but the flakes must be mixed first with denatured alcohol. The latter is ideal for preparing only as much of the solution as you need for a particular project. Both types of shellac are available in a variety of shades, ranging from dark brown and orange to blonde and white.

APPLICATION SEQUENCE

1. Either buy or prepare a 1- or 2-pound-cut shellac and apply two or three wash coats to the working surface. Brush the finish on quickly and evenly, with the grain. Avoid overlapping the brush strokes.

2. Let the surface dry, typically for two hours, then sand with a self-lubricating 360- or 400-grit sandpaper. Remove sanding particles.

3. Brush on another coat, using a 3-pound-cut shellac, and sand.

4. Apply three or more coats with a five-pound-cut shellac, sanding between coats.

5. Allow 24 to 72 hours of drying time before rubbing out the finish (page 130).

LACQUER

APPLICATION SEQUENCE

1. Dilute the lacquer with a retarding solvent as specified by the manufacturer. A 50 percent dilution is typical for the first two coats that are applied. The retarder keeps the lacquer from drying too quickly.

2. Coat the workpiece with the finish using a soft, long-bristled brush. Work at a 45° angle to the surface and brush with the grain. Do not overlap brushstrokes.

3. Let the lacquer dry (typically 2 hours), then sand with a self-lubricating 360- to 400-grit sandpaper. Remove sanding particles.

4. Repeat steps 1 to 3, using a slightly more concentrated lacquer solution.

5. Apply at least two or three additional coats. Avoid brushing undiluted lacquer on the surface; you should add at least a small amount of retarder to the lacquer.

6. Let the finish dry for at least 24 hours before rubbing it out *(page 130)*.

Lacquer has been used as a protective finish for wood furniture in the Far East for more than 2000 years, but it did not become popular in the West until the 17th Century. The first lacquers used during China's Chou dynasty were derived from natural resins; today's products are formulated synthetically.

When brushing lacquer onto a surface, be sure to use a brush with bristles set in rubber, otherwise the solvent in the finish may cause the tool to shed. A lacquer topcoat hardens to a clear and durable finish, making it a good choice for furniture that might be exposed to water or high heat.

Unlike polyurethanes and varnishes, which form separate layers with each new coating, each application of lacquer dissolves the previous coats to create a single film. Finishers usually try to limit themselves to four coats of lacquer in addition to the first two heavily diluted coats. This is because the thicker a lacquer finish is built up, the greater the risk of cracking.

APPLYING A FINISH

Wiping on a finish

Wiping is the best way of applying a drying oil. Wet a clean cloth or a sponge with the finish and wipe a thin coat of the liquid onto the surface *(right)*. Make sure you cover the wood completely. Let the finish soak into the wood for several minutes, then use another clean cloth to wipe away the excess. Check the manufacturer's instructions for drying times, and apply subsequent coats the same way.

Padding on a finish
Some finishing products, called padding finishes, are made to be padded onto a surface. Use a piece of linen and some wool to make a pad as you would for French polishing *(page 132)*. Pour a little of the finish on the pad, then tap it against the palm of your hand to get the pad uniformly damp. Wipe the pad along the surface following the direction of the grain *(left)*. Overlap your strokes until you have covered the entire work-piece and the surface has a smooth, glossy sheen. Consult the manufacturer's instructions for drying times, then apply subsequent coats. Padding finishes usually require several applications.

Brushing on a finish
Set the workpiece slightly above your work surface so you can cover the wood right to the bottom without slopping finish on the table. For a shop-made stand, prop the corners on wood blocks with small nails driven through them. If you are using a bristle brush, dip about one-third of the bristle length in the finish and brush along the grain leaving behind thin, even coats *(right)*. Resist the temptation to spread the finish thickly or the liquid will run, sag, or pool. To avoid air bubbles and lap marks on the surface, use as few brushstrokes as possible. Use tweezers to remove stray bristles from the finish before it has a chance to dry. A foam brush will cut down on the problem of lap marks.

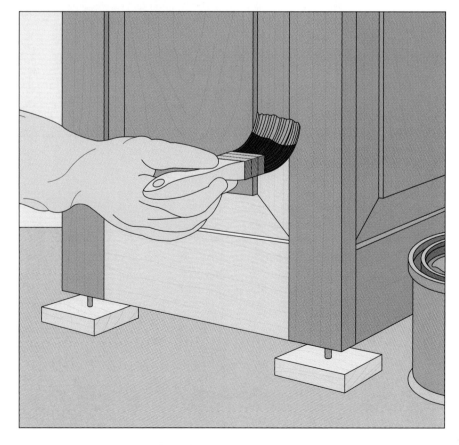

RUBBING OUT A FINISH

Once a finish is fully cured, it is time to rub it out. Rubbing out a finish with an abrasive, such as pumice or rottenstone, imparts a look suggestive of brushed brass and leaves the wood smooth and silky to the touch. The notion of abrading a meticulously applied finish may seem incongruous, but the final coat of finish on a piece of furniture seldom leaves the surface clear and perfectly smooth. You will often find the surface speckled with imperfections. Some evidence of brush bristle marks may also be visible, and rubbing out will remove these flaws.

The first step in the rubbing out process is to level the surface, and then to buff it to the desired sheen. The finish you end up with—satin or gloss—depends on the grit of the abrasive. A coarser-grit compound like pumice, a powdered form of volcanic rock, will impart a satin finish. A finer-grit compound, such as rottenstone, creates a glossier look.

The only potential problem associated with this process is the risk of rubbing through the finish. Always work carefully, especially near edges.

Fitted with a lamb's wool buffing bonnet, a random-orbit sander serves as an electric polisher, rubbing out the finish and buffing the topcoat to a high-gloss sheen.

RUBBING OUT A FINISH WITH A TRADITIONAL ABRASIVE

1 Applying the lubricant
If you choose to rub out a finish with pumice and rottenstone, you will need to use a lubricant. Water and oils, like kerosene and mineral oil, are the most commonly used lubricants. Although water speeds up the process and does not leave any oily residue, avoid using it on shellac; it will turn the finish white. Dip the tips of your fingers in a bowl of the lubricant and sprinkle several drops on the surface to be rubbed out *(right)*. Wear rubber gloves if you are using oil as a lubricant.

2 Abrading the surface

Shake a little pumice onto the surface, then begin lightly abrading the surface with a felt block *(right)*. Start near a corner and move in a straight line along the edge, keeping every stroke parallel to the wood grain and rubbing the surface with moderate pressure from one end to the other, working back and forth until you reach the other edge. If you do not have a felt block, wrap a piece of burlap around a scrap of wood. Continue rubbing the surface until a slurry of pumice and lubricant forms. Use a soft cloth to wipe off a small area of the surface periodically to inspect the finish. You want to make certain that you are not rubbing through the topcoat.

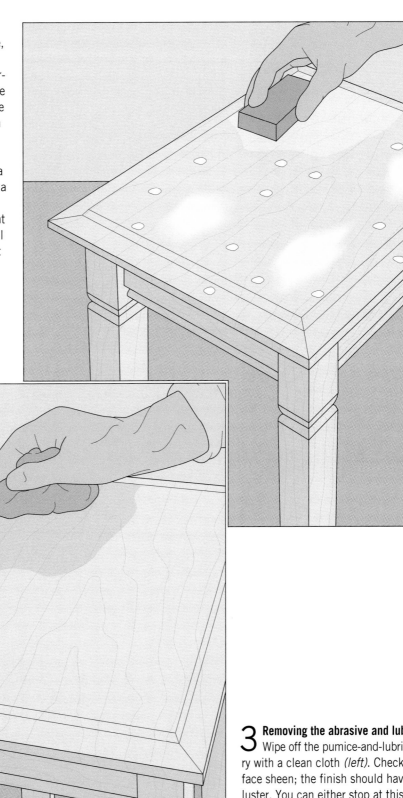

3 Removing the abrasive and lubricant

Wipe off the pumice-and-lubricant slurry with a clean cloth *(left)*. Check the surface sheen; the finish should have a satin luster. You can either stop at this point or repeat the process using a finer-abrasive rottenstone to obtain a glossier sheen.

ANTIQUE FINISHES

This section explains how to duplicate a couple of time-honored finishes that you may find on better-quality antiques. Originating in an era when time, labor, and materials were cheap and the finisher's art was rife with jealously guarded secrets, these finishes demand a fair amount of elbow grease and patience as well as deft technique.

French polishing involves padding on shellac with a cloth, as shown below. The result is a lustrous, almost three-dimensional finish. Although a French polish does not stand up to water, alcohol, or heat, it is relatively easy to repair. The materials required include wool and linen rags, shellac flakes and denatured alcohol mixed to a 2½- to 3½-pound cut, mineral oil, pumice, and polishing compound. The process consists of several steps performed over three days: On the first day, a coat of oil is applied to the piece and the excess is wiped off. Then the pores are filled with pumice. On the second day, several coats of shellac are padded on to build up the finish. On the third day, the oil film is removed with a clean cloth.

Gilding, the Renaissance art of laying a thin layer of a metal such as gold, silver, or bronze on a surface, is another classic wood-finishing technique, used mainly on ornamental moldings. Supplies for gilding are available at most finish suppliers. As shown starting on page 136, one method of gilding involves applying metal leaf to wood—a tricky process, requiring experience and a steady hand. An alternative and simpler technique is to apply metal powder to a prepared surface, as shown in the photo at left.

The gilded surface of a mirror frame is being spot-refinished with a brush and an alchemical mix of paint primer, adhesive, and powdered gold. A coat of red automotive primer is brushed onto the surface first, followed by an application of size—a special water-based adhesive. Lastly, the powdered gold is lightly and adroitly sprinkled on the glue, creating an invisible repair.

FRENCH POLISHING

1 Making a French polishing pad
Take a piece of wool roughly 3 inches square and fold the corners toward the center, stretching the wool with each fold. Then squeeze the wool pad into an oval and add a few drops of 2½- to 3½-pound-cut shellac. Disperse the shellac throughout the wool by crumbling the pad in your hand, then place it in the middle of a single thickness of coarse linen. Add several drops of alcohol to the pad *(right)*.

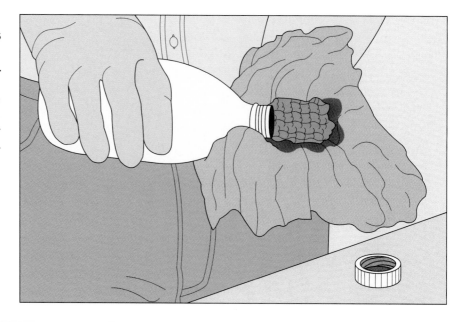

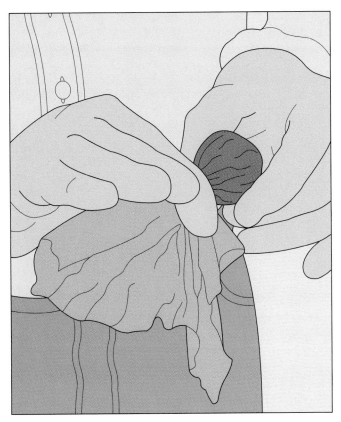

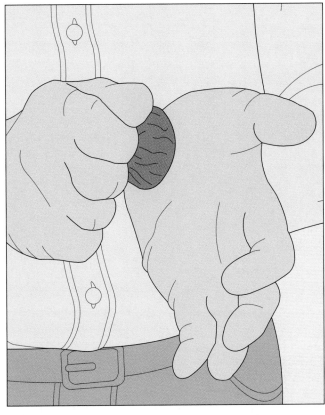

2 Preparing the pad for French polishing
Gather the linen around the ball of wool and twist the linen until the pad is held firmly in place *(above, left)*. Then tap the pad against the palm of your hand to spread the shellac and alcohol and form a flat surface *(above, right)*. If the pad is too wet, squeeze out the excess liquid. (When not in use, the pad should be stored moist in an airtight container to prevent it from stiffening.)

SHOP TIP

Making a pumice dispencer
Some finishers use a salt shaker to sprinkle on pumice for French polishing *(page 134)*. You can also fashion a more traditional dispenser. Pour a small amount of pumice into a piece of linen. Fold the material over and tie the top with a small piece of string to form a ball. To use the dispenser, shake the bag, sifting a small amount of pumice through the cloth and onto the wood.

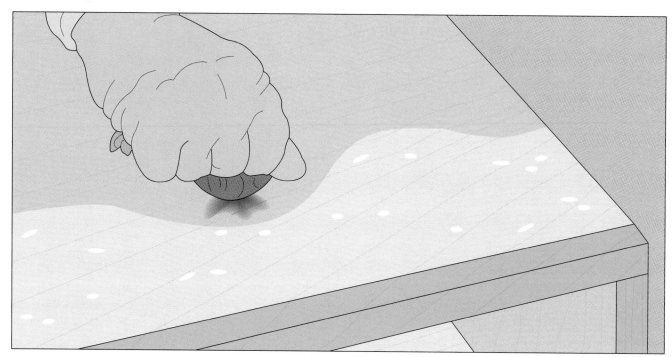

3 Filling the pores

Apply a sealer coat of shellac with a brush and allow it to dry. (This can be done before making the pad.) Then sprinkle pumice on the workpiece and shake a small amount on the pad. Grip the pad tightly between your fingers and thumb and work the pumice into the wood with any of the strokes shown in the diagram at right; choose the one that proves most comfortable. Keep the pad moving while it is on the surface to prevent the alcohol on the pad from leaving a mark in the finish *(above)*. Pay particular attention to the edges to avoid leaving them untouched. At first, the pumice will sound scratchy as you rub. The more the pores fill, the less scratchy the pumice will sound. Continue to pad, occasionally sprinkling on fresh pumice and adding more alcohol, until the pores are completely filled and the surface has a matte look. Depending on the size of the workpiece, this procedure may require 30 minutes or more. After filling the pores, set the workpiece aside for a day.

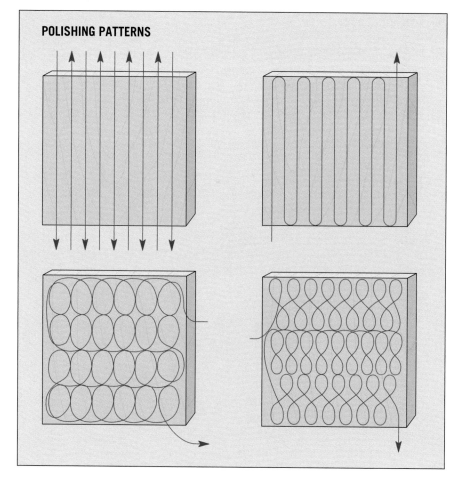

POLISHING PATTERNS

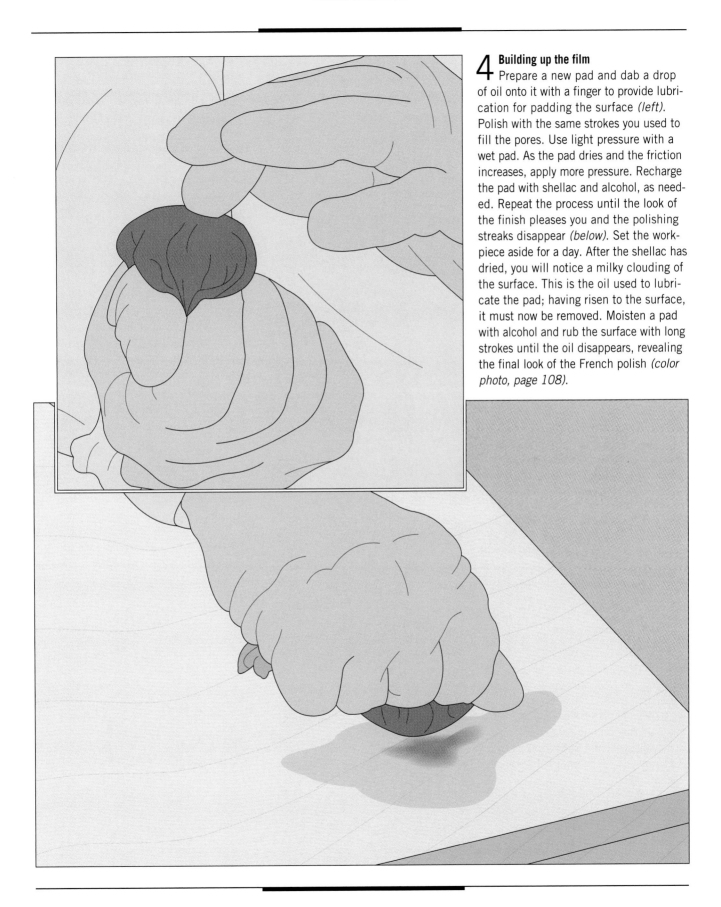

4 Building up the film
Prepare a new pad and dab a drop of oil onto it with a finger to provide lubrication for padding the surface *(left)*. Polish with the same strokes you used to fill the pores. Use light pressure with a wet pad. As the pad dries and the friction increases, apply more pressure. Recharge the pad with shellac and alcohol, as needed. Repeat the process until the look of the finish pleases you and the polishing streaks disappear *(below)*. Set the workpiece aside for a day. After the shellac has dried, you will notice a milky clouding of the surface. This is the oil used to lubricate the pad; having risen to the surface, it must now be removed. Moisten a pad with alcohol and rub the surface with long strokes until the oil disappears, revealing the final look of the French polish *(color photo, page 108)*.

GILDING

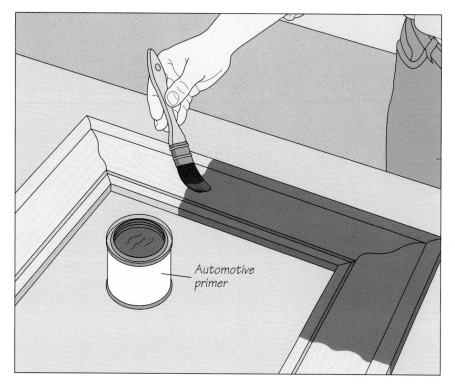

Automotive primer

1 Applying the base coat
The gilding method shown here involves preparing the workpiece with primer, spreading on adhesive, and then applying the leaf. In traditional gilding, an undercoat of gesso—a mixture of chalk and animal hide glue—is applied to the surface, followed by a base coat of clay. You can substitute a coating of primer paint, such as red automotive primer, for both the undercoat and base coat. The primer will seal the wood, prepare the surface for the size *(step 2)*, and impart a warm, aged color to the metal you will apply in step 3. Using a paintbrush, apply the primer to the surfaces to be gilded, working parallel to the wood grain *(left)*. Let the primer dry, smooth the surface with fine-grit sandpaper, and brush on another coat, if necessary.

2 Brushing on the size
Once the final coat of primer is dry and smooth, apply the size—a special water-based adhesive used for gilding. Brush on a coat of the glue the same way you applied the primer *(right)* and allow it to cure. Drying times for different brands of size vary, so check the manufacturer's instructions; some types take minutes to cure, while others require up to 12 hours. Once the size is tacky, it is ready for the metal leaf.

Size

3 Applying the metal leaf

Metal leaf is generally available in sheets about 5½ inches square. The sheets are sold in packs of 10 separated by paper. To handle the leaves use a special fine-bristled brush, available at any gilding supplier. To facilitate lifting a leaf from the pack, gently rub the brush against your hair to charge it with static electricity, then touch the brush bristles to the top leaf to pick it up. Lower the leaf onto the workpiece, placing it over the surface to be gilded. Work slowly; the slightest draft can cause the thin leaf to float off the brush. With the leaf in place, use a soft, 1-inch-wide sable brush to stroke the leaf down *(right)*. Starting at one edge, press the leaf down on all the flat surfaces and crevices. Should the leaf rip as you try to stretch it into a crevice, simply fill the gap with a new piece.

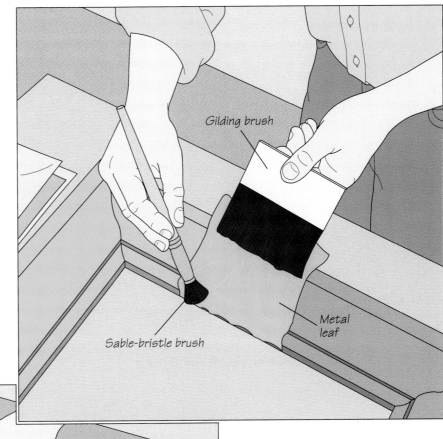

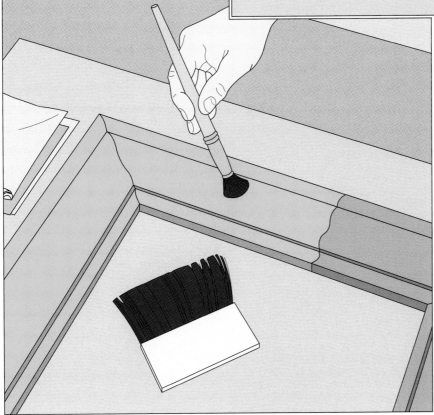

4 Burnishing the leaf

As each leaf is laid down, pass the sable brush back and forth over it *(left)*. The brush will remove any areas of overlap, since the leaf only adheres to the size. The result will be a seamless, shiny surface.

One of the challenges of restoring furniture is making sections that you have repaired or surfaces that you have refinished look as old—and battered—as the surrounding wood. Over the years, several techniques have been developed to "antique" furniture by distressing the wood—everything from

burying the piece for months in the backyard to firing at it with a 12-gauge shotgun. While unscrupulous dealers will even go to these extreme lengths to make a new piece appear old, such drastic measures seldom fool anyone but casual observers.

Most experienced furniture restorers contend that more benign antiquing techniques have their place in the craft of woodworking. A few well-placed dents, for example, will "age" wood more effectively than beating it with a chain. As you restore a piece and consider ways to make the surface reflect the age of the

A pickled finish can give a chair the time-worn appearance of a vintage antique.

surrounding wood, try to imagine how the piece would have been distressed naturally. A worn front stretcher on a chair would be an expected sign of age, since it would be exposed to occasional abuse from feet resting on it; a rear stretcher would not. The tips below describe several popular antiquing methods used by furniture restorers.

Hardware provides the finishing touch to a piece of furniture. Ideally, it should reflect the age and style of the piece. If there is no hardware left on your furniture, you can do a little research to discover what is appropriate for the piece you own and then order what you need from a store specializing in reproduction hardware. If you decide to use only original hardware, check out flea markets and antique dealers.

COMMON TECHNIQUES FOR ANTIQUING FURNITURE

ANTIQUING TIPS

• Worm holes can be imitated by piercing the wood with either an ice pick, a small drill bit, or a nail head filed to a sharp point. With worm holes—as with real estate—location is a key consideration. Rather than penetrating the wood surface indiscriminately, select areas likely to have been worm-infested, such as near the base of a leg. An easier, but less controlled, way to imitate worm holes involves spattering the surface with dark paint, such as raw umber or black. Simply hold the end of a stiff-bristled brush near the surface and run a stick across the bristles.

• To imitate the time-worn look of old wax-and-dirt buildup, try shading the surface with a dark-colored glaze and wiping it off quickly. This leaves the stain only in the pores and crevices of the surface. Use a varnish with pigment suspended in it, or a commercial stain followed by a coat of tinted varnish.

• Pickling, or liming, is used to impart an aged and weathered look to light-colored wood. Traditionally, woodworkers have pickled furniture with such chemicals as nitric acid, lye, and lime. But as shown above and on page 139, you can achieve

comparable results by applying a coat of white paint, pigmented white shellac, or white glaze to the workpiece.

• If you cannot find authentic hardware for a piece, you can make modern pieces such as handles, pulls, and hinges appear older by heating them with a propane torch. To avoid burning yourself, hold the hardware in locking pliers or clamp it to a noncombustible work surface. Cool by dipping it in cold water.

• As an alternative to the common but extreme practice of distressing wood by beating it with chains, try using a rasp and a file to carefully wear away selected parts of a workpiece, such as the edge of a desk or table, or the front stretcher of chair. To help you select a location, imagine which areas would normally receive wear and tear.

• Leaving furniture outdoors and bathed in water to soak up stains, although commonly done, may do more harm that good. The piece may need to be brought indoors to dry for a long time, and its joints may weaken or fall apart, requiring disassembly and regluing. As an alternative, use this method only on replace-

ment parts before installing them in the piece. Some furniture restorers will leave a piece outdoors for a few months, only exposing the wood to the elements to age the wood. An even less drastic method—and one that takes less time—involves experimenting with different dyes and pigments until you achieve the desired effect.

• To imitate the effects of the natural aging of wood, you can try burning the surface with a blowtorch or with a chemical, such as lye. This will soften or—with fire—even char the more porous earlywood on the surface, leaving the denser latewood intact. By scraping the softened or charred wood away with a stiff brush, you will ridge the surface. If you choose to try this method, exercise caution; wood is combustible, after all. With chemical burning, remember to neutralize the agent once it has done its work. Lye, for example, is neutralized with vinegar. Otherwise, the chemical will continue to eat away at the wood, causing more damage than you intended.

• A simple way to give furniture an aged look is to replace any visible nails or screws with dowels.

APPLYING A PICKLED FINISH

1 Applying the base coat
Use a rag to spread white paint or stain on the surfaces to be pickled. While the paint is still wet, wipe off the bulk of it with a burlap rag, leaving a whitish glaze on flat surfaces and streaks of white in crevices and carvings *(left)*. Let the stain dry. If the effect is too pronounced, abrade the surface with 220-grit sandpaper until you obtain the look you want.

2 "Aging" the surface
To give the surface an antique appearance, use a rag to rub a mixture of rottenstone and paste wax over the surface *(below)*. Wipe off the excess with a burlap rag, taking care to leave some residue in the crevices and carvings.

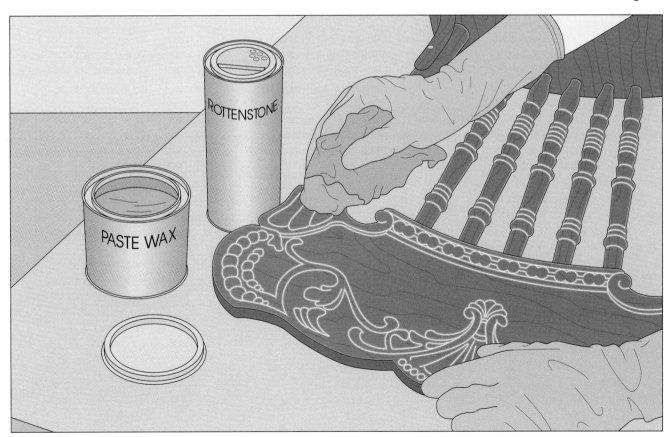

GLOSSARY

A-B

Alligatoring: A widespread pattern of narrow cracks in a finish giving the appearance of an alligator's hide.

Aniline dye: A lightfast, permanent synthetic dye derived from coal tars; soluble in water, alcohol, or oil.

Bleach: A liquid that chemically alters wood, lightening its color.

Brou de noix: A natural wood stain made from the husks of walnuts and water.

Butterfly key joint: A joint featuring a double wing-shaped hardwood key glued into a recess to strengthen a split tabletop or chair seat.

C-D-E

Carcase: The box-like body of a piece of furniture.

Countersink: Drilling a hole that allows a screw head to lie flush with or slightly below the surface of a workpiece.

Crazing: The tendency of a finish to fracture erratically as it dries; results from solvent incompatibility.

Denatured alcohol: An ethyl-alcohol-based solvent added to shellac flakes to produce liquid shellac; also used to dissolve and strip off a shellac finish.

Distressing: A finishing technique that involves adding scratches, dents, and other blemishes to the wood or topcoat to simulate the effects of age and wear.

Drying oil: One of a group of organic oils that hardens when exposed to air; the two common examples are tung oil and boiled linseed oil.

F-G-H-I-J

Featherboard: A piece of wood with thin, flexible fingers or "feathers" along one end used to press a workpiece securely against the fence or table of a power tool.

Fiber rush: Twisted kraft paper used to produce a rush seat; a modern alternative to traditional, rattan-plant rush seating.

French polishing: A traditional finish typically built up with many layers of shellac to produce a deep, lustrous sheen.

Gel stain: A blend of pigments and dyes in a gel that becomes liquid when stirred.

Gilding: A traditional method of applying gold leaf to furniture; artificial gold leaf made from a bronze alloy can be used as a substitute.

Graining: A decorative finishing technique in which a specific grain pattern is replicated.

Hide glue: Any of several types of glue made from animal hides that are heated before use and then harden upon cooling; traditionally used in older furniture.

K-L-M-N

Kerf: A cut made in wood by a saw blade.

Lacquer: A tough, clear synthetic finish usually derived from nitrocellulose; dries quickly to a flat or glossy finish.

Lightfast: Describes a stain or dye that does not readily fade after prolonged exposure to light.

Linseed oil: A traditional finish derived from flaxseed; the "double boiled" variety offers good protection and has a lustrous sheen.

Methylated spirits: A powerful chemical solvent made from purified wood alcohol used to strip a finish from a workpiece.

Methylene chloride: The active ingredient in most strong paint and varnish strippers.

Mineral spirits: A petroleum-based solvent commonly used for thinning various finishes and for cleaning application tools.

Mortise: A rectangular, round, or oval hole cut into a piece of wood, usually to accept a tenon.

NGR stain: Abbreviation of non-grain-raising stain. NGR stains are made from aniline dyes in a waterless solution of methanol and petroleum distillates; they are designed to avoid raising the grain of wood.

O-P-Q

Oxalic acid: A medium-strength bleach, often sold as "deck brightener."

Padding: A technique for wiping on a finish with a cloth pad.

Petroleum distillate: A solvent made from distilling petroleum; naphtha and mineral spirits are common examples.

Pigment: Finely ground, colored particles of earth or metallic oxides suspended in a liquid to create a stain or a tint for protective finishes.

Pilot hole: A hole drilled into a workpiece to prevent splitting when a screw is driven; usually made slightly smaller than the threaded section of the screw.

Plain-sawn veneer: Veneer that has been sawn so the wide surfaces are tangent to the annual growth rings.

Pumice: A volcanic rock that is ground to a powdery consistency for use as an abrasive.

R-S

Rail: The horizontal member of a frame-and-panel assembly. See *stile*.

Rottenstone: A fine abrasive made from pulverized limestone used to rub out finishes to a high gloss; texture is finer than that of pumice. Also used as an abrasive to remove blemishes from a finish.

Rubbing out: The process of abrading a topcoat to level the surface and add a sheen to the finish.

Shellac: A clear finish derived from the natural secretions of the lac beetle; sold ready to use or in flakes, which are then mixed with denatured alcohol.

Shellac stick: A stick of solid shellac sometimes blended with wax; melted and allowed to harden, it fills in gouges, dents, and other blemishes in a finish or wood surface. Available in various colors to match specific wood species.

Slurry: A fine paste-like mixture of lubricant and abrasive formed when rubbing out a finish.

Sodium hypochlorite: A type of bleach used to remove aniline dyes from wood.

Solvent: A liquid used to dissolve another substance; examples are turpentine, mineral spirits, lacquer thinner, and water.

Spanish windlass: A loop of rope twisted and tightened like a tourniquet; used to apply pressure when conventional clamping setups would be awkward.

Spline: A thin piece of wood that fits into mating grooves cut in two workpieces, reinforcing the joint between them.

Stile: The vertical member of a frame-and-panel assembly. See *rail*.

Stripping agent: A chemical product used to remove paint and finishes from furniture.

Substrate: A piece of plywood, softwood, or hardwood used as a core in veneering.

T-U-V-W-X-Y-Z

Tack cloth: A cloth dampened with an oil-and-varnish mixture or with water; used to remove sanding particles from wood surfaces.

Tannic acid: A naturally occuring acid found in wood; changes color when exposed to certain chemicals.

Tearout: The tendency of a blade or cutter to tear the fibers of the wood it is cutting, leaving ragged edges on the workpiece.

Template: A pattern used with a power tool to produce copies of the pattern.

Tenon: A protrusion on the end of a workpiece that fits into a mortise.

Tung oil: A water-resistant drying oil derived from the seeds of the tung tree; available in pure, modified, and polymerized forms. Also known as China wood oil.

Varnish: A clear finish made with synthetic oils that excels at resistance to water and alcohol.

Water-based finish: A product in which the solvent is primarily water.

Wet/dry sandpaper: A fine-grit sandpaper that can be used dry or with a lubricant.

Wood filler: A putty product used for repairing surface damage in wood, or a paste used for filling open grain.

INDEX

ACKNOWLEDGMENTS

The editors wish to thank the following:

RESTORING BASICS
Adjustable Clamp Co., Chicago, IL; Albert Constantine & Son Inc., Bronx, NY;
American Conservation Consortium, Fremont, NH; Great Neck Saw Mfrs. Inc. (Buck Bros. Division),
Millbury, MA; Hancock Shaker Village, Pittsfield, MA; Les Decorateurs de Montreal Ltée, Montreal, Que.;
Minotaur Workshop, Montreal, Que.; Mohawk Finishing Products, Montreal, Que.; Sandvik Saws and
Tools Co., Scranton, PA; Stanley Tools, Division of the Stanley Works, New Britain, CT;
Winterthur Museum, Winterthur, DE; Woodcraft Supply Corp., Parkersburg, WV

REPAIRING JOINTS
Adjustable Clamp Co., Chicago, IL; American Tool Cos., Lincoln, NE; Delta International
Machinery/Porter-Cable, Guelph, Ont.; Dewalt Industrial Tool Co., Hampstead, MD;
Grand Central Inc., Montreal, Que.; Great Neck Saw Mfrs. Inc. (Buck Bros. Division), Millbury, MA;
Sears, Roebuck and Co., Chicago, IL

MAJOR REPAIRS
Adjustable Clamp Co., Chicago, IL; American Tool Cos., Lincoln, NE; Black & Decker/Elu Power Tools,
Towson, MD; Delta International Machinery/Porter-Cable, Guelph, Ont.; Dewalt Industrial Tool Co.,
Hampstead, MD; Elastoproxy, Saint Eustache, Que.; Grand Central Inc., Montreal, Que.;
H.H. Perkins, Woodbridge, CT; Intermares Trading Co., Lindenhurst, NY; Sandvik Saws and Tools Co.,
Scranton, PA; Sherbrooke Upholstering, Sherbrooke, Que.; Skil Power Tools Canada, Markham, Ont.;
Steiner/Lamello A.G. Switzerland/Colonial Saw Co., Kingston, MA

RESTORATION TECHNIQUES
Adjustable Clamp Co., Chicago, IL; Dewalt Industrial Tool Co., Hampstead, MD;
Grand Central Inc., Montreal, Que.; Great Neck Saw Mfrs. Inc. (Buck Bros. Division), Millbury, MA;
Pianoforte, Montreal, Que.; Richards Engineering Co. Ltd., Vancouver, B.C.;
Sandvik Saws and Tools Co., Scranton, PA; Stanley Tools, Division of the Stanley Works, New Britain, CT;
Tool Trend Ltd., Concord, Ont.; Williams and Hussey Machine Co. Inc., Wilton, NH

SURFACE AND FINISH REPAIRS
Grand Central Inc., Montreal, Que.; Mohawk Finishing Products, Montreal, Que.;
Pianoforte, Montreal, Que.

REFINISHING
Adjustable Clamp Co., Chicago, IL; Delta International Machinery/Porter-Cable, Guelph, Ont.;
Grand Central Inc., Montreal, Que.; Lee Valley Tools, Ottawa, Ont.;
Les Decorateurs de Montreal Ltée, Montreal, Que.; Mohawk Finishing Products, Montreal, Que.;
Olde Mill Cabinet Shoppe, York, PA; Pianoforte, Montreal, Que.

The following persons also assisted in the preparation of this book:

Philippe Arnoldi, Elizabeth Cameron, Art Chesmer, Nabil Codsi, Lorraine Doré, Luc Germain,
Johanne Lapointe, Pauline Van Sertima, W. N. Steltzer, Jr

PICTURE CREDITS